**LIVING THROUGH
THE COLD WAR**

Living Through Watergate

Other Books in the Living Through the Cold War series:

Living Through Watergate

Debra A. Miller, Book Editor

GREENHAVEN PRESS

An imprint of Thomson Gale, a part of The Thomson Corporation

Detroit • New York • San Francisco • New Haven, Conn. • Waterville, Maine • London • Munich

Bonnie Szumski, *Publisher*
Helen Cothran, *Managing Editor*

© 2006 Thomson Gale, a part of The Thomson Corporation.

Thomson and Star logo are trademarks and Gale and Greenhaven Press are registered trade-marks used herein under license.

For more information, contact:
Greenhaven Press
27500 Drake Rd.
Farmington Hills, MI 48331-3535
Or you can visit our Internet site at http://www.gale.com

LIBRARY OF CONGRESS CATALOGING-IN-PUBLICATION DATA

Living through Watergate / Debra A. Miller, book editor.
p. cm. -- (Living through the Cold War)
Includes bibliographical references and index.
ISBN 0-7377-2917-1 (hardcover : alk. paper)
1. Watergate Affair, 1972–1974. 2. Nixon, Richard M. (Richard Milhous), 1913–1994--Resignation from office. 3. United States--Politics and government--1969–1974. 4. Watergate Affair, 1972–1974--Sources. 5. United States--Politics and government--1969–1974--Sources. I. Miller, Debra A. II. Series.
E860.L58 2006
973.924--dc22

2006017069

Printed in the United States of America
10 9 8 7 6 5 4 3 2 1

Contents

Chapter 2: The Watergate Scandal Unfolds

Chapter 3: The Legacy of Watergate

Foreword

A t the midpoint of the Cold War, in early 1968, U.S. television viewers saw surprising reports from Vietnam, where American ground troops had been fighting since 1965. They learned that South Vietnamese Communist rebels, known as the Vietcong, had attacked unexpectedly throughout the country. At one point Vietcong insurgents engaged U.S. troops and officials in a firefight at the very center of U.S. power in Vietnam, the American embassy in South Vietnam's capital, Saigon. Meanwhile, thousands of soldiers and marines faced a concerted siege at Khe Sanh, an isolated base high in central Vietnam's mountains. Their adversary was not the Vietcong, but rather the regular North Vietnamese army.

Reporters and U.S. citizens quickly learned that these events constituted the Tet Offensive, a coordinated attack by Vietnamese Communists that occurred in late January, the period of Tet, Vietnam's new year. The American public was surprised by the Tet Offensive because they had been led to believe that the United States and its South Vietnamese allies were winning the war, that Vietcong forces were weak and dwindling, and that the massive buildup of American forces (there were some five hundred thousand U.S. troops in Vietnam by early 1968) ensured that the south would remain free of a Communist takeover. Since 1965, politicians, pundits, and generals had claimed that massive American intervention was justified and that the war was being won. On a publicity tour in November 1967 General William Westmoreland, the American commander in Vietnam, had assured officials and reporters that "the ranks of the Vietcong are thinning steadily" and that "we have reached a point where the end begins to come into view." President Lyndon B. Johnson's advisers, meanwhile, continually encouraged him to publicly emphasize "the light at the end of the tunnel."

Ordinary Americans had largely supported the troop buildup in Vietnam, believing the argument that the country was an important front in the Cold War, the global effort to stop the spread of communism that had begun in the late 1940s. Communist regimes already held power in nearby China, North Korea, and in northern Vietnam; it was deemed necessary to hold the line in the south not only to prevent communism from taking hold there but to prevent other nations from falling to communism throughout Asia. In 1965 polls showed that 80 percent of Americans believed that intervention in Vietnam was justified despite the fact that involvement in this fight would alter American life in numerous ways. For example, young men faced the possibility of being drafted and sent to fight—and possibly die—in a war thousands of miles away. As the war progressed, citizens watched more and more of their sons—both draftees and enlisted men—being returned to the United States in coffins (approximately fifty-eight thousand Americans died in Vietnam). Antiwar protests roiled college campuses and sometimes the streets of major cities. The material costs of the war threatened domestic political reforms and America's economic health, offering the continuing specter of rising taxes and shrinking services. Nevertheless, as long as the fight was succeeding, a majority of Americans could accept these risks and sacrifices.

Tet changed many minds, suggesting as it did that the war was not, in fact, going well. When CBS news anchor Walter Cronkite, who was known as "the most trusted man in America," suggested in his broadcast on the evening of February 27 that the Vietnam War might be unwinnable and could only end in a stalemate, many people wondered if he might be right and began to suspect that the positive reports from generals and politicians might have been misleading. It was a turning point in the battle for public opinion. Johnson reportedly said that Cronkite's expressions of doubt signaled the loss of mainstream America's support for the war. Indeed, after Tet more and more people joined Cronkite in wondering whether fighting this obscure enemy in an isolated country halfway around the world was worth the cost—whether it was a truly important front in the Cold War. They made their views known through demonstrations and opinion polls, and politicians were forced to respond. In a dramatic and unexpected turn of events, Johnson declined to run for reelection in 1968, stating that his involvement in the political campaign would detract from his efforts to negotiate a peace agreement with North Vietnam. His successor, Richard Nixon, won the election after promising to end the war.

The Tet Offensive and its consequences provide strong examples of how the Cold War touched the lives of ordinary Americans. Far from being an abstract geopolitical event, the Cold War, as Tet reveals, was an ever-present influence in the everyday life of the nation. Greenhaven Press's Living Through the Cold War series provides snapshots into the lives of ordinary people during the Cold War, as well as their reactions to its major events and developments. Each volume is organized around a particular event or distinct stage of the Cold War. Primary documents such as eyewitness accounts and speeches give firsthand insights into both ordinary peoples' experiences and leaders' decisions. Secondary sources provide factual information and place events within a larger global and historical context. Additional resources include a detailed introduction, a comprehensive chronology, and a thorough bibliography. Also included are an annotated table of contents and a detailed index to help the reader locate information quickly. With these features, the Living Through the Cold War series reveals the human dimension of the superpower rivalry that defined the globe during most of the latter half of the twentieth century.

Introduction

During three years in the early 1970s Americans lived through one of the most notorious political scandals in U.S. history. More than thirty years later Watergate still stands as the country's most significant political scandal—one that involved abuses of power at the highest levels of government and tested America's most cherished democratic values.

A Quiet Beginning

The Watergate story began quietly on June 17, 1972, when the Associated Press reported that five men—later identified as Bernard Barker, Virgilio González, Eugenio Martínez, James W. McCord Jr., and Frank Sturgis—were arrested trying to break into the offices of the Democratic National Committee at the office complex of the Watergate Hotel in Washington, D.C. This was actually the second time the burglars had broken into the complex. The first time they bugged the phones, and on June 17, 1972, they broke in again to try to fix the malfunctioning listening devices. The burglars were discovered by a security guard, Frank Wills, who noticed that the lock on an office door had been taped open. Wills removed the tape but called the police after he noticed it was soon retaped.

Just two days later, on June 19, 1972, two young men, then unknown reporters Bob Woodward and Carl Bernstein from the *Washington Post*, reported that one of the burglars, James W. McCord Jr., was a former Central Intelligence Agency (CIA) employee who was working as a paid security coordinator for President Nixon's reelection committee—the Committee to Reelect the President (CRP), later commonly referred to as CREEP. Another link to the White House was established when Bernard Barker's notebook was found to contain a phone number for E. Howard Hunt, a White House employee. John N. Mitchell, head of CREEP, quickly denied that McCord or the other burglars were operating on the committee's behalf in the burglary. A short time later, in August 1972, Nixon declared that no one then employed in his administration was involved in the Watergate break-in.

Despite the denials, however, the FBI began an investigation into the matter. In addition, Woodward and Bernstein continued to report on Watergate throughout the summer, often relying on a secret source inside the government known as "Deep Throat," who helped the team by confirming information they learned from other sources. Their aggressive journalism throughout this and later time periods helped to keep the matter of Watergate in the public eye. Yet nothing emerged from these investigations to prevent Nixon from being reelected by a landslide victory against Democratic candidate George McGovern on November 7, 1972.

More Ties to the White House

Just two months after Nixon's reelection, in January 1973, the five burglars went to trial before Judge John Sirica in the U.S. district court in Washington, D.C., on charges of conspiracy, burglary, and illegal wiretapping. Joining them were two White House employees, E. Howard Hunt and G. Gordon Liddy, who were found to be in communication with the burglars. Five of the defendants pleaded guilty and the two who did not, McCord and Liddy, were convicted. The Watergate scandal took on even more significance on March 23, 1973, when McCord sent a letter to Sirica charging that the defendants had been pressured into pleading guilty by top White House officials and that perjury had been committed during the trial. McCord's revelations marked a critical turning point in the Watergate affair, because they implicated high-level White House officials in an effort to obstruct justice and hide the administration's involvement.

Further investigation by the FBI showed that the Watergate bugging was part of a broad program of political spying and dirty tricks run by White House officials. Investigators learned, for example, that the Watergate crime was undertaken on behalf of CREEP under the direction of Hunt and Liddy, both of whom worked for a White House Special Investigation Unit—nicknamed "the Plumbers"—set up by White House aide John Ehrlichman. The Plumbers had a history of trying to discredit the Democratic Party as well as protesters opposed to U.S. involvement in the war in Vietnam. One 1971 Plumbers mission that later became famous was a break-in at the office of the psychiatrist of former Pentagon employee Daniel Ellsberg in an attempt to prevent Ellsberg from leaking confidential information about the Vietnam War (called the Pentagon Papers) to the press. Investigators also discovered that the Watergate defendants were being paid by CREEP to remain silent and that this money came from a CREEP "slush fund" financed by illegal corporate donations. The burglary and cover-up were now directly linked to the White House.

In an attempt to defuse the growing scandal, Nixon addressed the nation in a nationally televised speech on April 30, 1973. In the speech Nixon implicitly claimed to be innocent of any involvement. He said he was shocked by the burglary and disappointed to learn about the involvement of his reelection committee. He said he immediately ordered an investigation and was repeatedly assured that no one in his administration was involved. Nixon said he learned new information in March that led him to believe that some of the charges were true and that there was a cover-up. In an effort to preserve the integrity of his administration, Nixon announced the resignation of top White House aides H.R. (Bob) Haldeman and John Ehrlichman, White House counsel to the President John Dean, and Attorney General Richard Kleindienst. Responding to Democratic demands for an impartial prosecutor, Nixon also announced the appointment of a new attorney general—Elliot Richardson—who was instructed to undertake a complete investigation. On May 18, 1973, Richardson selected Archibald Cox, a well-respected attorney and Harvard law professor, to be special prosecutor for the U.S. Justice Department's Watergate case.

The Watergate Cover-Up Linked to the President

Also in mid-May 1973, the Senate Watergate committee—officially called the Senate Select Committee on Presidential Campaign Activities—began hearings on Watergate. Chaired by the folksy but well-respected senator Sam Ervin, a Democrat from North Carolina, the committee heard from many witnesses during the summer of 1973, and the testimony was broadcast on television gavel-to-gavel, riveting the nation.

On June 25–June 29, 1973, the Senate committee heard testimony from one of its most critical witnesses—White House counsel John Dean. Dean testified that Nixon talked to him repeatedly about cover-up activities, including matters such as executive clemency, hush money for the Watergate burglars, and ways to prevent political damage from Justice Department investigations and congressional hearings. Dean also described a climate of fear within the White House, stemming from the president himself, that led Nixon staffers to use illegal tactics to undermine political opponents, attack antiwar protestors, punish critics in the press, and collect intelligence on political enemies. Dean's testimony, given under a grant of immunity from criminal prosecution, shocked the country because it directly contradicted Nixon's claims that he knew nothing about a Watergate cover-up.

A short time later another development occurred that many observers think was the key to unraveling the Watergate scandal. On July 16, 1973, Alexander P. Butterfield, a deputy assistant to the president, revealed to the Senate Watergate committee that all presidential conversations in the Oval Office were tape-recorded using a secret taping system installed for historical purposes. Butterfield's testimony had huge significance: If such tapes existed they would clearly show whether Nixon was implicated in the Watergate crime and cover-up.

The Battle over the Presidential Tapes

President Nixon, however, spent the next three months fighting all efforts by Cox and the Senate Watergate committee to force him to hand over the tapes. In his second speech to the nation about Watergate, Nixon on August 15, 1973, explained his rationale for refusing to surrender them. He asserted that presidents must not be subject to court orders to produce documents and other evidence—a principle called "executive privilege." Producing the tapes, he said, would destroy the confidentiality of presidential conversations and prevent presidents from speaking freely and confidentially to aides. In the speech Nixon also again denied that he had any knowledge of a cover-up, and he urged the nation to abandon its obsession with Watergate.

Contending that Nixon had already waived executive privilege by allowing his aides to testify before Congress, however, Cox asked Sirica for an order instructing the White House to turn over the tapes, an order that was granted on August 29, 1973. Nixon appealed the order but lost. On October 12, 1973, the U.S. Court of Appeals for the District of Columbia ordered production of the tapes. Again, the White House refused.

Instead, on October 19, 1973, President Nixon proposed a compromise to end the tapes dispute—he would furnish a "summary" of the taped presidential conversations that would be verified by Senator John Stennis, a Democrat from Mississippi. Cox rejected the compromise, however, and planned to appeal the matter to the U.S. Supreme Court.

A Government Crisis

Before Cox could appeal, however, Nixon took an extraordinary and dramatic action that brought the country to the edge of a national crisis. In what was later known as the "Saturday Night Massacre," Nixon, on October 20, 1973, ordered Richardson to fire Cox. Richardson resigned rather than discharge Cox. Deputy Attorney General William D. Ruckelshaus was then asked to fire Cox, but he also refused to do so and resigned. Finally, Solicitor General Robert H. Bork, who became acting attorney general after Ruckelshaus's discharge, dismissed Cox. The president also announced that he was abolishing the special prosecutor's office and transferring its duties back to the Justice Department.

Nixon's decision to dismiss Cox quickly backfired. It unleashed a firestorm of criticism, set off a wave of public protests and a flood of letters to Congress and the White House, and prompted calls for the president to resign or be impeached and removed from office. Faced with the mounting government crisis and the threats of impeachment, Nixon on October 23, 1973, reversed himself, appointed a new special prosecutor, Leon Jaworski, and promised to submit the tapes to Sirica.

Struggles over the tapes continued, however. The White House claimed that two of the nine requested tapes—involving a telephone conversation between Nixon and his then campaign manager John Mitchell three days after the Watergate burglary and an April 15, 1973, conversation between Nixon and his former counsel John Dean—did not exist because those calls were never recorded. In addition, White House lawyers informed Sirica that part of another tape—eighteen-and-a-half minutes of a conversation between Nixon and his chief of staff, H.R. Haldeman, three days after the burglary—was blank. Rose Mary Woods, Nixon's loyal secretary, claimed she accidentally erased the tape, but a panel of experts examining the tapes reported that the eighteen-minute gap was instead caused by at least five separate and deliberate erasing and rerecording operations.

Concerned about the possible destruction of evidence, Jaworski requested and Sirica issued (on April 18, 1974) a new, broader subpoena for tapes of sixty-four presidential conversations, covering a period from June 20, 1972, to June 4, 1973. Nixon responded by steadfastly resisting turning over more tapes or evidence either to Congress or to the special prosecutor. On April 30, 1974, the White House attempted another compromise solution, providing Congress with twelve hundred pages of edited transcripts of his taped conversations with key aides. The transcripts failed to satisfy demands for the tapes themselves, but they revealed the private Nixon in a very unflattering light—as a man who frequently used profanity, sought to block congressional probes, and tried to deceive the special Watergate prosecutor.

Finally, in a decision released on July 24, 1974, in a case known as *United States v. Nixon*, the U.S. Supreme Court ruled 8-0 that Nixon must turn over the sixty-four tape recordings to the special prosecutor. The Court rejected the president's claims of executive privilege, explaining that such a privilege exists only for matters dealing with diplomatic or national security secrets—claims that were not advanced by Nixon. Much to the relief of the public and many in government, Nixon agreed to comply with the Court's ruling and produce the tapes.

The March Toward Impeachment

As the battle over the presidential tapes raged, the U.S. House of Representatives authorized the House Judiciary Committee to consider whether Nixon should be impeached for his involvement in the Watergate affair. In late July 1974 the committee scheduled public hearings on the issue, and House members hotly debated the impeachment issue. One of the most famous speeches at the hearings was given by Representative Barbara Jordan, a well-respected Democrat from Texas. Jordan argued that a president is impeachable if he subverts the Constitution, and she said the evidence against Nixon rose to this level because it showed that he tried to cover up the Watergate crime and in various ways attempted to obstruct the criminal justice system.

By the time the hearings ended on July 30, 1974, the House Judiciary Committee had adopted three articles of impeachment against Nixon. The first article charged the president with obstruction of the investigation of the Watergate break-in. The second article charged Nixon with misuse of power and violation of his oath of office. The third article charged the president with attempting to impede the impeachment process by failing to comply with House subpoenas for tapes and records. At least seven Republicans on the committee voted with the committee's Democrats for impeachment. The articles were referred to the full House of Representatives, but it was not clear whether there would be enough votes in the House to impeach Nixon.

The "Smoking Gun" Evidence

Under enormous political and public pressure, Nixon, on July 30, 1974, released twenty of the sixty-four Watergate-related tapes. A few days later, on August 5, 1974, Nixon also released tapes of three conversations he had with his top aide, H.R. Haldeman, in the days immediately after the Watergate burglary. One of these tapes contained a conversation held on June 23, 1972, in which Nixon directed White House aide H.R. Haldeman to order the CIA to halt the FBI investigation of the Watergate affair. This tape soon became known as the "smoking gun" because it confirmed not only that Nixon knew of the cover-up of the Watergate scandal, but that he had in fact directed it.

Because of this incontrovertible evidence against Nixon, the eleven Republicans on the House Judiciary Committee who voted against impeachment said they were now in favor of impeachment. Nixon was also advised by key Republican senators on August 7, 1974, that there were now enough votes in the Senate to convict him. At this point it became clear that unless Nixon resigned, he would be impeached by the House of Representatives and removed from office by the Senate.

Realizing he had no option other than resigning or being removed from office, on the evening of August 8, 1974, Nixon addressed the nation in a televised speech, announcing his resignation from the office of the president, effective at noon the following day, August 9, 1974. The next day Nixon departed the White House by helicopter. His resignation letter was delivered to Secretary of State Henry Kissinger at 11:35 A.M., and Vice President Gerald R. Ford was sworn in as president soon thereafter. The day was historic: Nixon was the first president ever to resign from office.

Shortly after being sworn into office on August 9, 1974, Ford spoke to the nation at 12:05 P.M. from the East Room of the White House. He asked Americans to support him and assured the nation that the "national nightmare" of Watergate had ended. About a month later, on September 8, 1974, Ford granted a broad pardon to Nixon, immunizing him from prosecution for any crimes he may have committed as president. Despite his resignation, without this pardon Nixon could have faced criminal prosecution for his participation in the Watergate cover-up. Although he still claimed innocence, Nixon accepted the pardon, an action that many took as an admission of guilt.

A Constitutional Crisis Averted

At the time of Nixon's resignation and during the years immediately afterward, Watergate was viewed as a shameful stain on the history of American politics. As more years passed, however, many people forgot the intensity of the events of the early 1970s and new generations of Americans hardly knew about the Watergate drama. Nixon, in the decades after his resignation, was even able to regain much of his dignity. He maintained contact with some later presidents and was praised for his work in the area of foreign policy, especially for his efforts to establish a new, friendlier relationship between the United States and China. He died of a stroke on April 22, 1994, and at his funeral, which was attended by former presidents and other notables, no one even mentioned Watergate by name.

Despite the softening of memories about Watergate, however, constitutional scholars say that the scandal has great historical importance. If Nixon had not reversed his decision to halt the special prosecutor's progress, the American public might have rebelled against what they saw as a corrupt president. If Nixon had refused to obey the Supreme Court's order to hand over presidential tapes, it would have pitted two branches of government against each other in a way that would have challenged the essence of America's Constitution—the separation of powers of the three-branch system of government, in which each branch acts as a check against the excesses of the others. Indeed, Watergate tested the very roots of American democracy and brought the country to the brink of a constitutional crisis.

The lessons of Watergate remain as important today as in 1974. The president was not above the law; the constitutional system of checks and balances worked; and power was transferred to a new president without violence.

LIVING THROUGH
THE COLD WAR

Official Statements on Watergate

President Nixon
Accepts Responsibility

Richard M. Nixon

Months after the June 17, 1972, Watergate burglary, an FBI in-
vestigation revealed that the break-in and bugging were part of
a larger campaign of political sabotage directed by top White
House aides. In response to growing political pressure, President
Richard M. Nixon gave his first nationally televised speech about
Watergate on April 30, 1973. In the speech, Nixon took responsi-
bility for the Watergate affair but implicitly denied any personal
knowledge or involvement. Promising to get to the bottom of the
matter, Nixon announced the resignation of Attorney General
Richard Kleindienst and top White House aides Bob Haldeman
and John Erlichman and White House counsel John Dean. Re-
sponding to Democrats' demands for an impartial prosecutor in
the affair, Nixon also announced the appointment of a new at-
torney general—Elliot Richardson—who was instructed to un-
dertake a complete investigation. Nixon assured his television
audience, "Justice will be pursued, fully, fairly, and impartially,
no matter who is involved."

I want to talk to you tonight from my heart on a subject of deep concern to every American.

In recent months, members of my Administration and officials of the Committee for the Re-election of the President—including some of my closest friends and most trusted aides—have been charged with involvement in what has come to he known as the Watergate affair. These include charges of illegal activity during and preceding the 1972 Presidential election and charges that responsible officials participated in efforts to cover up that illegal activity.

Richard M. Nixon, televised speech given from the White House, April 30, 1973.

The inevitable result of these charges has been to raise serious questions about the integrity of the White House itself. Tonight I wish to address those questions.

Initial Response to Watergate

Last June 17 [1972], while I was in Florida trying to get a few days, rest after my visit to Moscow, I first learned from news reports of the Watergate break-in. I was appalled at this senseless, illegal action, and I was shocked to learn that employees of the Re-election Committee were apparently among those guilty. I immediately ordered an investigation by appropriate Government authorities. On September 15 [1972], as you will recall, indictments were brought against seven defendants in the case.

As the investigations went forward, I repeatedly asked those conducting the investigation whether there was any reason to believe that members of my Administration were in any way involved. I received repeated assurances that there were not. Because of these continuing reassurances, because I believed the reports I was getting, because I had faith in the persons from whom I was getting them, I discounted the stories in the press that appeared to implicate members of my Administration or other officials of the campaign committee.

Until March of this year [1973], I remained convinced that the denials were true and that the charges of involvement by members of the White House Staff were false. The comments I made during this period, and the comments made by my Press Secretary in my behalf, were based on the information provided to us at the time we made those comments. However, new information then came to me which persuaded me that there was a real possibility that some of these charges were true, and suggesting further that there had been an effort to conceal the facts both from the public, from you, and from me.

As a result, on March 21 [1973], I personally assumed the responsibility for coordinating intensive new inquiries into the matter, and I personally ordered those conducting the investigations to get all the facts and to report them directly to me, right here in this office.

I again ordered that all persons in the Government or at the Re-election Committee should cooperate fully with the FBI, the prosecutors, and the grand jury. I also ordered that anyone who refused to cooperate in telling the truth would be asked to resign from Government service. And, with ground rules adopted that would preserve the basic constitutional separation of powers between the Congress and the Presidency, I directed that members of the White House Staff should appear and testify voluntarily under oath before the Senate committee which was investigating Watergate.

I was determined that we should get to the bottom of the matter, and that the truth should be fully brought out—no matter who was involved.

Resignation of Top White House Aides

At the same time, I was determined not to take precipitate action and to avoid, if at all possible, any action that would appear to reflect on innocent people. I wanted to be fair. But I knew that in the final analysis, the integrity of this office—public faith in the integrity of this office—would have to take priority over all personal considerations.

Today [April 30, 1973], in one of the most difficult decisions of my Presidency, I accepted the resignations of two of my closest associates in the White House—Bob Haldeman, John Ehrlichman—two of the finest public servants it has been my privilege to know.

I want to stress that in accepting these resignations, I mean to leave no implication whatever of personal wrongdoing on their part, and I leave no implication tonight of implication on the part of others who have been charged in this matter. But in matters as sensitive as guarding the integrity of our democratic process, it is essential not only that rigorous legal and ethical standards be observed but also that the public, you, have total confidence that they are both being observed and enforced by those in authority and particularly by the President of the United States. They agreed with me that this move was necessary in order to restore that confidence.

Because Attorney General Kleindienst—though a distinguished public servant, my personal friend for 20 years, with no personal involvement whatever in this matter—has been a close personal and professional associate of some of those who are involved in this case, he and I both felt that it was also necessary to name a new Attorney General.

The Counsel to the President, John Dean, has also resigned.

Appointment of a New Attorney General

As the new Attorney General, I have today named Elliot Richardson, a man of unimpeachable integrity and rigorously high principle. I have directed him to do everything necessary to ensure that the Department of Justice has the confidence and the trust of every law-abiding person in this country.

I have given him absolute authority to make all decisions bearing upon the prosecution of the Watergate case and related matters. I have instructed him that if he should consider it appropriate, he has the authority to name a special supervising prosecutor for matters arising out of the case.

Whatever may appear to have been the case before, whatever improper activities may yet be discovered in connection with this whole sordid affair, I want the American people, I want you, to know beyond the shadow of a doubt that during my term as President, justice will be pursued fairly, fully, and impartially, no matter who is involved. This office is a sacred trust and I am determined to be worthy of that trust.

Accepting Responsibility

Looking back at the history of this case, two questions arise:

- How could it have happened?

- Who is to blame?

Political commentators have correctly observed that during my 27 years in politics I have always previously insisted on running my own campaigns for office.

But 1972 presented a very different situation. In both domestic and foreign policy, 1972 was a year of crucially important decisions, of intense negotiations, of vital new directions, particularly in working toward the goal which has been my overriding concern throughout my political career—the goal of bringing peace to America, peace to the world.

That is why I decided, as the 1972 campaign approached, that the Presidency should come first and politics second. To the maximum extent possible, therefore, I sought to delegate campaign operations, to remove the day-to-day campaign decisions from the President's office and from the White House. I also, as you recall, severely limited the number of my own campaign appearances.

Who, then, is to blame for what happened in this case?

For specific criminal actions by specific individuals, those who committed those actions must, of course, bear the liability and pay the penalty.

For the fact that alleged improper actions took place within the White House or within my campaign organization, the easiest course would be for me to blame those to whom I delegated the responsibility to run the campaign. But that would be a cowardly thing to do.

I will not place the blame on subordinates—on people whose zeal exceeded their judgment and who may have done wrong in a cause they deeply believed to be right.

In any organization, the man at the top must bear the responsibility. That responsibility, therefore, belongs here, in this office. I accept it. And I pledge to you tonight, from this office, that I will do everything in my power to ensure that the guilty are brought to justice and that such abuses are purged from our political processes in the years to come, long after I have left this office.

Faith in the Judicial System

Some people, quite properly appalled at the abuses that occurred, will say that Watergate demonstrates the bankruptcy of the American political system. I believe precisely the opposite is true. Watergate represented a series of illegal acts and bad judgments by a number of individuals. It was the system that has brought the facts to light and that will bring those guilty to justice—a system that in this case has included a determined grand jury; honest prosecutors; a courageous judge, John Sirica; and a vigorous free press.

It is essential now that we place our faith in that system—and especially in the judicial system. It is essential that we let the judicial process go forward, respecting those safeguards that are established to protect the innocent as well as to convict the guilty. It is essential that in reacting to the excesses of others, we not fall into excesses ourselves.

It is also essential that we not be so distracted by events such as this that we neglect the vital work before us, before this Nation, before America, at a time of critical importance to America and the world. . . .

The Need for Campaign Reform

But we cannot achieve [the nation's] goals unless we dedicate ourselves to another goal.

We must maintain the integrity of the White House, and that integrity must be real, not transparent. There can be no whitewash at the White House.

We must reform our political process—ridding it not only of the violations of the law but also of the ugly mob violence and other inexcusable campaign tactics that have been too often practiced and too readily accepted in the past, including those that may have been a response by one side to the excesses or expected excesses of the other side. Two wrongs do not make a right.

I have been in public life for more than a quarter of a century. Like any other calling, politics has good people and bad people. And let me tell you, the great majority in politics—in the Congress, in the Federal Government, in the State government—are good people. I know that it can be very easy, under the intensive pressures of a campaign, for even well-intentioned people [to] fall into shady tactics—to rationalize this on the grounds that what is at stake is of such importance [to] the Nation that the end justifies the means. And both of our great parties have been guilty of such tactics in the past.

In recent years, however, the campaign excesses that have occurred on all sides have provided a sobering demonstration of how far this false doctrine can take us. The lesson is clear: America, in its political campaigns, must not again fall into the trap of letting the end, however great that end is, justify the means.

I urge the leaders of both political parties, I urge citizens, all of you, everywhere, to join in working toward a new set of standards, new rules and procedures to ensure that future elections will be as nearly free of such abuses as they possibly can be made. This is my goal. I ask you to join in making it America's goal.

Hope for the Future

When I was inaugurated for a second time this past January 20, I gave each member of my Cabinet and each member of my senior White House Staff a special 4-year calendar, with each day marked to show the number of days remaining to the Administration. In the inscription on each calendar, I wrote these words: "The Presidential term which begins today consists of 1,461 days—no more, no less. Each can be a day of strengthening and renewal for America; each can add depth and dimension to the American experience. If we strive together, if we make the most of the challenge and the opportunity that these days offer us, they can stand out as great days for America, and great moments in the history of the world."

I looked at my own calendar this morning up at Camp David [the presidential retreat] as I was working on this speech. It showed exactly 1,361 days remaining in my term. I want these to be the best days in America's history, because I love America. I deeply believe that America is the hope of the world. And I know that in the quality and wisdom of the leadership America gives lies the only hope for millions of people all over the world that they can live their lives in peace and freedom. We must be worthy of that hope, in every sense of the word. Tonight, I ask for your prayers to help me in everything that I do throughout the days of my Presidency to be worthy of their hopes and of yours.

God bless America and God bless each and every one of you.

The Supreme Court Rules That Nixon Must Turn Over Presidential Tapes

John P. MacKenzie

After Alexander P. Butterfield, a presidential assistant, revealed in testimony before the Senate Watergate Committee that all presidential conversations in the Oval Office were secretly tape-recorded, a battle ensued among the president and the courts and Congress over release of the presidential tapes. President Nixon, however, steadfastly resisted turning over most of the requested tapes, either to the Congress or to the Watergate special prosecutor. Finally, in a decision released on June 24, 1974, in a case known as United States v. Nixon, *the U.S. Supreme Court ruled 8-0 that Nixon had to turn over sixty-four tape recordings subpoenaed by Special Prosecutor Leon Jaworski. The Court rejected the president's claims of executive privilege, explaining that such a privilege exists only for matters dealing with diplomatic or national security secrets—claims that Nixon did not make. John P. MacKenzie, a staff reporter for the* Washington Post, *described the Court's decision in this July 25, 1974, article. Nixon ultimately agreed to comply with the Court's ruling to produce the tapes.*

The Supreme Court ruled yesterday [July 24, 1974], unanimously, and definitively, that President Nixon must turn over tape recordings of White House conversations needed by the Watergate special prosecutor for the trial of the President's highest aides.

Ordering compliance with a trial subpoena "forthwith," the court rejected Mr. Nixon's broad claims of unreviewable executive privilege and said they "must yield to the demonstrated, specific need for evidence in a pending criminal trial."

The President said he was "disappointed" by the decision but said he would comply. His lawyer said the time-consuming process of collecting and indexing the tapes would begin immediately.

Chief Justice Warren E. Burger delivered the historic judgment in a packed and hushed courtroom. His 31-page opinion drew heavily on both the great cases of the court's past, as well as the pro-prosecution edicts of a court dominated by Nixon appointees.

Only a few times in its history has the court grappled with such large assertions of governmental power. As in most of those encounters, the justices concluded that the judiciary must have the last word in an orderly constitutional system even though its view of the Constitution is "at variance with the construction given the document by another branch."

Implications for Impeachment

Brushing aside warnings by presidential lawyer James D. St. Clair that it was in an impeachment thicket, the court handed down its 8-to-0 ruling hours before the House Judiciary Committee was scheduled to open debate on proposed articles of impeachment.

One justice, William H. Rehnquist, disqualified himself because of his previous association with former Attorney General John N. Mitchell in the Justice Department.

The decision itself had implications for the impeachment proceedings. Although the court said it was not concerned with "congressional demands for information," the ruling weakened the White House legal argument against Judiciary Committee subpoenas.

Calls for prompt compliance with the Supreme Court decision came from Congress. A few voices were heard for slowing down the impeachment drive long enough to explore the remote hope that Congress could obtain the tapes from U.S. District Court Judge John J. Sirica or Watergate Special Prosecutor Leon Jaworski.

Jaworski, who has denied St. Clair's charge that his office is a mere conduit of evidence for pro-impeachment forces, was restrained in expressing satisfaction at the ruling. "It doesn't leave any doubt in anyone's mind," he said.

Claims of Executive Privilege Rejected

Only one of St. Clair's arguments came close to persuading the justices. The court declared, in its most extensive discussion of the issue to date, that executive privilege is "constitutionally based" even though it is not specifically mentioned in the Constitution.

But while communication between the President and his advisers is "presumptively privileged," the court said that this presumption can be outweighed by the demonstrated needs of the judicial process.

The court recognized a privilege for matters dealing with diplomatic or national security secrets, but stressed that federal judges may inspect such material in chambers in the course of selecting evidence the prosecutor should have.

No such security claims have been advanced in the current dispute over subpoenaed tapes and documents covering 64 conversations—most of which implicate the President himself in the Watergate cover-up conspiracy, according to Jaworski— between June, 1972, and April 26 of this year [1974].

Any national security arguments must now be advanced directly to Judge Sirica, whose May 20 order to produce the material for his inspection was affirmed in all respects.

Producing the Tapes

The judge initially gave St. Clair 11 days to produce the original tapes and documents along with an index showing what portions the White House contended were irrelevant, together with copies of 20 tapes for which Mr. Nixon published edited White House transcripts on April 30.

This screening process may consume most of the seven weeks that remain before the Sept. 9 trial of John N. Mitchell, H.R. Haldeman, John D. Ehrlichman and other Nixon confidants. Evidence introduced at that trial would be available to Congress, too late for the scheduled House impeachment vote but in time for a Senate trial if that occurs.

If White House lawyers disagree with any ruling by Judge Sirica on relevance or executive privilege, they are free to attempt piecemeal delaying appeals to the U.S. Court of Appeals, but the high court indicated that the judge's rulings should not be lightly overturned.

St. Clair in a statement . . . at the Western White House in San Clemente indicated that collecting and organizing the tapes for submission to Judge Sirica had not yet begun. In a brief statement he told newsmen the process "will begin forthwith."

During the oral argument July 8, Justice Thurgood Marshall suggested that the process should have begun some time ago. St. Clair said he hadn't started because he did not expect to lose the appeal from Judge Sirica's order. . . .

No Person Is Above the Law

Burger's opinion [indicated] that the evidence at trial may link Mr. Nixon to the alleged conspiracy. If that happens, Mr. Nixon's taped statements are easily admissible as evidence against the defendants. Burger said Judge Sirica did not err in his preliminary, pre-trial estimate that the evidence was admissible and therefore should be produced now.

Burger said the pre-trial test of executive privilege was especially appropriate in this case because, although no President is "above the law," it would be "unseemly" to frame the dispute as a case of contempt for violating a court order.

The impact of the court's decision was increased by the fact that it was delivered by Burger, appointed to the nation's top judicial post by President Nixon.

Equally impressive was the court's unanimity on every issue in the case—a tricky question of the court's jurisdiction, the enforcement of the subpoena under conventional criminal law standards and the merits of the executive privilege controversy.

Jaworski's Unique Position

The issue of jurisdiction, considered by some legal scholars to be St. Clair's strongest point, also raised a storm in Congress over whether the administration had reneged on its pledge giving Jaworski independence and the right to take the President to court over disputes on executive privilege.

St. Clair argued that the pledges, contained in published Justice Department regulations, did not and could not guarantee that the courts would have the legal power to decide contests between President Nixon and his executive branch subordinate, Jaworski.

Jaworski replied that this argument would make a "mockery" of his role, which was worked out to prevent a repetition of the "Saturday night massacre" firing last October [1973] of his predecessor, Archibald Cox.

Burger easily disposed of St. Clair's argument. He said the unique job security and authority granted to Jaworski under regulations having "the force of law" made the case far more significant than the mere "intra-branch" squabble St. Clair said it was.

Even assuming the President once had the power to order Jaworski fired, Burger said, he denied himself that authority with the regulations. And while "it is theoretically possible" to revoke the regulations, the attorney general "has not done so. So long as this regulation remains in force the executive branch is bound by it, and indeed the United States as the sovereign composed of the three branches is bound to respect and to enforce it."

This reasoning also appears to mean it was illegal to fire Cox last fall, since a similar regulation was in force then. A decision in U.S. District Court here [in Washington, D.C.] declaring the Cox firing illegal is currently on appeal.

Although Burger did not mention it, it is widely assumed that any move now to dismiss Jaworski would result in another "firestorm" of protest and hasten President Nixon's impeachment.

Burger said that looking beneath the formal titles of the parties and their formal relationship within the same branch of government, the case was clearly "the kind of controversy courts traditionally resolve," especially since it comes up in the course of a criminal trial in a federal court.

Tapes Admissible Under Criminal Law Rules

Moving to the propriety of the subpoena under ordinary criminal law rules, Burger said Judge Sirica clearly acted within his powers in finding the requested evidence relevant to the prosecution, probably admissible as evidence and sufficiently specific to avoid being characterized as part of a "fishing expedition."

Burger said Jaworski was able to show where each of the 64 conversations fits into the prosecution's case aided by White House logs, testimony from last summer's Watergate hearings and grand jury evidence.

Burger said St. Clair's "most cogent objection to the admissibility of the taped conversations" was that they were "hearsay" statements by individuals "who will not be subject to cross-examination" at trial.

It was here that the chief justice appeared to acknowledge that President Nixon could be treated as a co-conspirator for purposes of admitting his statements in evidence, even if the

President was correct in contending that the grand jury lacked power to label him a conspirator in a formal vote. Burger said:

"Declarations by one defendant may also be admissible against other defendants upon a sufficient showing, by independent evidence of a conspiracy among one or more other defendants and the declarant and if the declarations at issue were in furtherance of that conspiracy."

Burger said a blend of deference to the trial judge and to the President was appropriate in handling this delicate question. Trial judges are afforded wide discretion in ordinary cases, he noted, but added that reviewing courts "should be particularly meticulous to insure that the standards" of criminal law have been correctly applied "where a subpoena is directed to a President of the United States.

"The justices have examined the record, including some grand jury material that is still under seal, and they are satisfied that Judge Sirica met the standards in evaluating the question of probable admissibility," Burger said.

Executive Privilege Denied

Finally, Burger reached the heart of the dispute, and he quickly found that President Nixon was wrong in arguing that courts must honor without question any presidential claim of executive privilege.

Burger repeatedly said the court had the utmost respect for the other branches of government but was obliged to reach its own judgment on whether the President's need for confidentiality was as great as the judiciary's need for the evidence.

Acknowledging that each branch of government "must initially interpret the Constitution and the interpretation of its powers by any branch is due great respect from the others," Burger then quoted and reaffirmed a classic phrase from the

1803 opinion of Chief Justice John Marshall in the case of *Marbury vs. Madison*:

"It is emphatically the province and duty of the judicial department to say what the law is."

Burger also acknowledged Jaworski's argument that "executive privilege" isn't mentioned in the Constitution although some enumerated privileges have been given restricted scope by the high court. But he accepted St. Clair's argument instead and declared that "certain powers and privileges flow from the nature of enumerated powers. The protection of the confidentiality of presidential communications has similar constitutional underpinnings."

But, said Burger, "when the privilege depends solely on the broad, undifferentiated claim of public interest in the confidentiality of such conversations, a confrontation with other values arises." Without a plea to protect military, diplomatic or national security secrets, he said, "we find it difficult to accept" the argument that confidentiality would be significantly diminished by a turnover.

"We cannot conclude," he said, "that advisers will be moved to temper the candor of their remarks by the infrequent occasions of disclosure because of the possibility that such conversations will be called for in the context of a criminal prosecution."

A Case for Impeachment

Barbara Jordan

On October 30, 1973, after details of the Watergate scandal were revealed in congressional testimony and Nixon battled to withhold tapes and other evidence from the courts and Congress, the House Judiciary Committee, chaired by Representative Peter W. Rodino Jr., a Democrat from New Jersey, began to consider impeaching Nixon. Members of the House debated the issue, with some urging an impeachment vote and others arguing that the evidence of Nixon's involvement in Watergate was thin. In a now famous speech given on the House floor on July 25, 1974, Representative Barbara Jordan, a Democrat from Texas, reminded her colleagues of the constitutional basis for impeachment. She noted that Founding Father James Madison, at the constitutional convention, had said, "A President is impeachable if he attempts to subvert the Constitution." Jordan argued that Nixon had attempted to subvert the Constitution because the evidence showed that he had urged his aides to commit perjury, had tried to cover up the Watergate burglary, and had attempted to compromise the process of criminal justice. A few days later the committee adopted three articles of impeachment against Nixon.

Today I am an inquisitor. I believe hyperbole would not be fictional and would not overstate the solemnness that I feel right now. My faith in the Constitution is whole, it is complete, it is total. I am not going to sit here and be an idle spectator to the diminution, the subversion, the destruction of the Constitution.

The Nature of Impeachment

[In the *Federalist Papers*, Alexander Hamilton wrote] "Who can so properly be the inquisitors for the nation as the representatives of the nation themselves?" "The subject of its juris-

Barbara Jordan, speech before the U.S. House of Representatives' Committee on the Judiciary, July 25, 1974.

diction are those offenses which proceed from the misconduct of public men." That is what we are talking about. In other words, the jurisdiction comes from the abuse of violation of some public trust. It is wrong, I suggest, it is a misreading of the Constitution for any member here to assert that for a member to vote for an article of impeachment means that that member must be convinced that the president should be removed from office. The Constitution doesn't say that. The powers relating to impeachment are an essential check in the hands of this body, the legislature, against and upon the encroachment of the executive. In establishing the division between the two branches of the legislature, the House and the Senate, assigning to the one the right to accuse and to the other the right to judge, the framers of this Constitution were very astute. They did not make the accusers and the judges the same person.

We know the nature of impeachment. We have been talking about it awhile now. "It is chiefly designed for the president and his high ministers" to somehow be called into account. It is designed to "bridle" the executive if he engages in excesses. [As Hamilton wrote in the *Federalist Papers*] "It is designed as a method of national inquest into the public men." The framers confined in the congress the power, if need be, to remove the president in order to strike a delicate balance between a president swollen with power and grown tyrannical, and preservation of the independence of the executive. The nature of impeachment is a narrowly channeled exception to the separation-of-powers maxim; the federal convention of 1787 said that. It limited impeachment to high crimes and misdemeanors and discounted and opposed the term "maladministration." "It is to be used only for great misdemeanors," so it was said in the North Carolina ratification convention. And in the Virginia ratification convention: "We do not trust our liberty to a particular branch. We need one branch to check the others."

The North Carolina ratification convention: "No one need be afraid that officers who commit oppression will pass with immunity."

"Prosecutions of impeachments will seldom fail to agitate the passions of the whole community," said Hamilton in the *Federalist Papers*, no. 65. "And to divide it into parties more or less friendly or inimical to the accused." . . .

The Grounds for Impeachment

Impeachment must proceed within the confines of the constitutional term "high crimes and misdemeanors."

Of the impeachment process, it was Woodrow Wilson who said that "nothing short of the grossest offenses against the plain law of the land will suffice to give them speed and effectiveness. Indignation so great as to overgrow party interest may secure a conviction; but nothing else can."

Common sense would be revolted if we engaged upon this process for insurance, campaign finance reform, housing, environmental protection, energy sufficiency, mass transportation. Pettiness cannot be allowed to stand in the face of such overwhelming problems. So today we are not being petty. We are trying to be big because the task we have before us is a big one.

This morning, in a discussion of the evidence, we were told that the evidence which purports to support the allegations of misuse of the CIA by the president is thin. We are told that that evidence is insufficient. What that recital of the evidence this morning did not include is what the president did know on June 23, 1972. The president did know that it was Republican money, that it was money from the Committee for the Re-election of the President which was found in the possession of one of the burglars arrested on June 17 [1972].

What the president did know on June 23 [1972] was the prior activities of E. Howard Hunt, which included his participation in the break-in of Daniel Ellsberg's psychiatrist.[1]. . .

We were further cautioned today that perhaps these proceedings ought to be delayed because certainly there would be new evidence forthcoming from the president. The committee subpoena is outstanding, and if the president wants to supply that material, the committee sits here.

The fact is that yesterday, the American people waited with great anxiety for eight hours, not knowing whether their president would obey an order of the Supreme Court of the United States.

The President's Actions Merit Impeachment

At this point I would like to juxtapose a few of the impeachment criteria with some of the president's actions.

Impeachment criteria: James Madison, from the Virginia ratification convention: "If the president be connected in any suspicious manner with any person and there be grounds to believe that he will shelter him, he may be impeached."

We have heard time and time again that the evidence reflects payment to the defendants of money. The president had knowledge that these funds were being paid and that these were funds collected for the 1972 presidential campaign.

We know that the president met with [assistant attorney general] Mr. Henry Petersen twenty-seven times to discuss matters related to Watergate and immediately thereafter met with the very persons who were implicated in the information Mr. Petersen was receiving and transmitting to the president.

1. In 1971 Ellsberg, a former military advisor, leaked the so-called Pentagon Papers to the press. The information in the papers on the execution of the Vietnam War by the Nixon and previous administrations reflected badly on the president, so Nixon tried to discredit Ellsberg by having Hunt break into the office of Ellsberg's psychiatrist, a Dr. Fielding, to find discrediting information. This break-in later became part of the Watergate cover-up scandal.

The words are "if the president be connected in any suspicious manner with any person and there be grounds to believe that he will shelter that person, he may be impeached."

Justice [Joseph] Story [of the U.S. Supreme Court, 1811–1845]: "Impeachment is intended for occasional and extraordinary cases where a superior power acting for the whole people is put into operation to protect their rights and rescue their liberties from violations."

We know about the Huston plan [a White House report on security operations that included illegal surveillance of left wing radicals]. We know about the break-in of the psychiatrist's office. We know that there was absolute, complete direction in August 1971 when the president instructed [presidential assistant John] Ehrlichman to "do whatever is necessary." This instruction led to a surreptitious entry into Dr. Fielding's office.

"Protect their rights." "Rescue their liberties from violation."

The South Carolina ratification convention impeachment criteria: those are impeachable "who behave amiss or betray their public trust."

Beginning shortly after the Watergate break-in and continuing to the present time, the president has engaged in a series of public statements and actions designed to thwart the lawful investigation by government prosecutors. Moreover, the president has made public announcements and assertions bearing on the Watergate case which the evidence will show he knew to be false.

These assertions, false assertions, impeachable, those who misbehave. Those who "behave amiss or betray their public trust."

The President Counsels His Aides to Commit Perjury

James Madison again at the Constitutional Convention: "A president is impeachable if he attempts to subvert the Constitution."

The Constitution charges the president with the task of taking care that the laws be faithfully executed, and yet the president has counseled his aides to commit perjury, willfully disregarded the secrecy of grand jury proceedings, concealed surreptitious entry, attempted to compromise a federal judge while publicly displaying his cooperation with the processes of criminal justice.

"A president is impeachable if he attempts to subvert the Constitution."

If the impeachment provision in the Constitution of the United States will not reach the offenses charged here, then perhaps that eighteenth-century Constitution should be abandoned to a twentieth-century paper shredder. Has the president committed offenses and planned and directed and acquiesced in a course of conduct which the Constitution will not tolerate? That is the question. We know that. We know the question. We should now forthwith proceed to answer the question. It is reason, and not passion, which must guide our deliberations, guide our debate, and guide our decision.

Nixon Resigns

Richard M. Nixon

On August 7, 1974, after the release of presidential tapes that clearly showed his involvement in the Watergate cover-up, Nixon met with three senior Republican congressmen who advised him that the chances of impeachment by the House of Representatives and removal from office by the Senate were almost certain. Realizing he had no options other than resigning or being removed from office, Nixon addressed the nation in a televised speech from the Oval Office on the evening of August 8, 1974. In the speech Nixon announced his resignation from the office of the president—an act, he said, he was taking for the good of the nation. The next day, Nixon left the White House, and Vice President Gerald R. Ford was sworn in as president soon thereafter. Nixon was the first and only U.S. president ever to resign from office.

This is the 37th time I have spoken to you from this office, where so many decisions have been made that shaped the history of this Nation. Each time I have done so to discuss with you some matter that I believe affected the national interest.

In all the decisions I have made in my public life, I have always tried to do what was best for the Nation. Throughout the long and difficult period of Watergate, I have felt it was my duty to persevere, to make every possible effort to complete the term of office to which you elected me.

In the past few days, however, it has become evident to me that I no longer have a strong enough political base in the Congress to justify continuing that effort. As long as there was such a base, I felt strongly that it was necessary to see the con-

Richard M. Nixon, televised resignation speech given from the White House, August 8, 1974.

stitutional process through to its conclusion; that to do otherwise would be unfaithful to the spirit of that deliberately difficult process and a dangerously destabilizing precedent for the future.

But with the disappearance of that base, I now believe that the constitutional purpose has been served, and there is no longer a need for the process to be prolonged.

The Best Interests of the Nation

I would have preferred to carry through to the finish, whatever the personal agony it would have involved, and my family unanimously urged me to do so. But the interests of the Nation must always come before any personal considerations.

From the discussions I have had with Congressional and other leaders, I have concluded that because of the Watergate matter I might not have the support of the Congress that I would consider necessary to back the very difficult decisions and carry out the duties of this office in the way the interests of the Nation would require.

I have never been a quitter. To leave office before my term is completed is abhorrent to every instinct in my body. But as President, I must put the interest of America first. America needs a full-time President and a full-time Congress, particularly at this time with problems we face at home and abroad.

To continue to fight through the months ahead for my personal vindication would almost totally absorb the time and attention of both the President and the Congress in a period when our entire focus should be on the great issues of peace abroad and prosperity without inflation at home.

Therefore, I shall resign the Presidency effective at noon tomorrow. Vice President Ford will be sworn in as President at that hour in this office.

Hastening the Healing Process

As I recall the high hopes for America with which we began this second term, I feel a great sadness that I will not be here in this office working on your behalf to achieve those hopes in the next two and a half years. But in turning over direction of the Government to Vice President Ford, I know, as I told the Nation when I nominated him for that office 10 months ago, that the leadership of America will be in good hands.

In passing this office to the Vice President, I also do so with the profound sense of the weight of responsibility that will fall on his shoulders tomorrow and, therefore, of the understanding, the patience, the cooperation he will need from all Americans.

As he assumes that responsibility, he will deserve the help and the support of all of us. As we look to the future, the first essential is to begin healing the wounds of this Nation, to put the bitterness and divisions of the recent past behind us, and to rediscover those shared ideals that lie at the heart of our strength and unity as a great and as a free people.

By taking this action, I hope that I will have hastened the start of that process of healing which is so desperately needed in America.

I regret deeply any injuries that may have been done in the course of the events that led to this decision. I would say only that if some of my judgments were wrong, and some were wrong, they were made in what I believed at the time to be the best interest of the Nation.

To those who have stood with me during these past difficult months, to my family, my friends, to many others who joined in supporting my cause because they believed it was right, I will be eternally grateful for your support.

And to those who have not felt able to give me your support, let me say I leave with no bitterness toward those who have opposed me because all of us, in the final analysis, have been concerned with the good of the country, however our judgments might differ.

President Richard Nixon resigns during an address to the nation from the Oval Office of the White House, August 8, 1974. AP Images.

So, let us all now join together in affirming that common commitment and in helping our new President succeed for the benefit of all Americans.

Achievements of This Administration

I shall leave this office with regret at not completing my term, but with gratitude for the privilege of serving as your President for the past five and a half years. These years have been a momentous time in the history of our Nation and the world. They have been a time of achievement in which we can all be proud, achievements that represent the shared efforts of the Administration, the Congress, and the people.

But the challenges ahead are equally great, and they, too, will require the support and the efforts of the Congress and the people working in cooperation with the new Administration.

We have ended America's longest war, but in the work of securing a lasting peace in the world, the goals ahead are even more far-reaching and more difficult. We must complete a structure of peace so that it will be said of this generation, our generation of Americans, by the people of all nations, not only that we ended one war but that we prevented future wars.

We have unlocked the doors that for a quarter of a century stood between the United States and the People's Republic of China.

We must now ensure that the one quarter of the world's people who live in the People's Republic of China will be and remain not our enemies but our friends.

In the Middle East, 100 million people in the Arab countries, many of whom have considered us their enemy for nearly 20 years, now look on us as their friends. We must continue to build on that friendship so that peace can settle at last over the Middle East and so that the cradle of civilization will not become its grave.

Together with the Soviet Union we have made the crucial breakthroughs that have begun the process of limiting nuclear arms. But we must set as our goal not just limiting but reducing and finally destroying these terrible weapons so that they cannot destroy civilization and so that the threat of nuclear war will no longer hang over the world and the people.

We have opened new relations with the Soviet Union. We must continue to develop and expand that new relationship so that the two strongest nations of the world will live together in cooperation rather than confrontation.

Around the world, in Asia, in Africa, in Latin America, in the Middle East, there are millions of people who live in terrible poverty, even starvation. We must keep as our goal turning away from production for war and expanding production for peace so that people everywhere on this earth can at last look forward in their children's time, if not in our own time, to having the necessities for a decent life.

Here in America, we are fortunate that most of our people have not only the blessings of liberty but also the means to live full and good and, by the world's standards, even abundant lives. We must press on, however, toward a goal of not only more and better jobs but of full opportunity for every American and of what we are striving so hard right now to achieve, prosperity without inflation.

The Nixon Legacy

For more than a quarter of a century in public life I have shared in the turbulent history of this era. I have fought for what I believed in. I have tried to the best of my ability to discharge those duties and meet those responsibilities that were entrusted to me.

Sometimes I have succeeded and sometimes I have failed, but always I have taken heart from what Theodore Roosevelt once said about the man in the arena, "whose face is marred by dust and sweat and blood, who strives valiantly, who errs and comes short again and again because there is not effort without error and shortcoming, but who does actually strive to do the deed, who knows the great enthusiasms, the great devotions, who spends himself in a worthy cause, who at the best knows in the end the triumphs of high achievements and who at the worst, if he fails, at least fails while daring greatly."

I pledge to you tonight that as long as I have a breath of life in my body, I shall continue in that spirit. I shall continue to work for the great causes to which I have been dedicated throughout my years as a Congressman, a Senator, a Vice President, and President, the cause of peace not just for

America but among all nations, prosperity, justice, and opportunity for all of our people.

There is one cause above all to which I have been devoted and to which I shall always be devoted for as long as I live.

When I first took the oath of office as President five and a half years ago, I made this sacred commitment, to "consecrate my office, my energies, and all the wisdom I can summon to the cause of peace among nations."

I have done my very best in all the days since to be true to that pledge. As a result of these efforts, I am confident that the world is a safer place today, not only for the people of America but for the people of all nations, and that all of our children have a better chance than before of living in peace rather than dying in war.

This, more than anything, is what I hoped to achieve when I sought the Presidency. This, more than anything, is what I hope will be my legacy to you, to our country, as I leave the Presidency.

To have served in this office is to have felt a very personal sense of kinship with each and every American. In leaving it, I do so with this prayer: May God's grace be with you in all the days ahead.

Our National Nightmare Has Ended

Gerald R. Ford

Shortly after being sworn into office by Chief Justice Warren E. Burger on August 9, 1974, President Gerald R. Ford spoke to the nation at 12:05 P.M. from the East Room of the White House. In the speech, Ford asked Americans to accept him as the nation's new president, urged Democrats and Republicans to work together, and promised to be honest and open in his presidency. He then assured the nation that the nightmare of Watergate was over. About a month later, on September 8, 1974, Ford granted a broad pardon to Nixon, immunizing him from prosecution for any crimes he may have committed as president.

The oath that I have taken is the same oath that was taken by George Washington and by every President under the Constitution. But I assume the Presidency under extraordinary circumstances never before experienced by Americans. This is an hour of history that troubles our minds and hurts our hearts.

Therefore, I feel it is my first duty to make an unprecedented compact with my countrymen. Not an inaugural address, not a fireside chat, not a campaign speech—just a little straight talk among friends. And I intend it to be the first of many.

A Plea for Support and Cooperation

I am acutely aware that you have not elected me as your President by your ballots, and so I ask you to confirm me as your President with your prayers. And I hope that such prayers will also be the first of many.

Gerald R. Ford, televised speech given from the White House, August 9, 1974.

If you have not chosen me by secret ballot, neither have I gained office by any secret promises. I have not campaigned either for the Presidency or the Vice Presidency. I have not subscribed to any partisan platform. I am indebted to no man, and only to one woman—my dear wife—as I begin this very difficult job.

I have not sought this enormous responsibility, but I will not shirk it. Those who nominated and confirmed me as Vice President were my friends and are my friends. They were of both parties, elected by all the people and acting under the Constitution in their name. It is only fitting then that I should pledge to them and to you that I will be the President of all the people.

Thomas Jefferson said the people are the only sure reliance for the preservation of our liberty. And down the years, Abraham Lincoln renewed this American article of faith asking, "Is there any better way or equal hope in the world?"

I intend, on Monday next, to request of the Speaker of the House of Representatives and the President pro tempore of the Senate the privilege of appearing before the Congress to share with my former colleagues and with you, the American people, my views on the priority business of the Nation and to solicit your views and their views. And may I say to the Speaker and the others, if I could meet with you right after these remarks, I would appreciate it.

Even though this is late in an election year, there is no way we can go forward except together and no way anybody can win except by serving the people's urgent needs. We cannot stand still or slip backwards. We must go forward now together.

To the peoples and the governments of all friendly nations, and I hope that could encompass the whole world, I pledge an uninterrupted and sincere search for peace. America will remain strong and united, but its strength will remain dedicated to the safety and sanity of the entire family of man, as well as to our own precious freedom.

Our Constitution Worked

I believe that truth is the glue that holds government together, not only our Government but civilization itself. That bond, though strained, is unbroken at home and abroad.

In all my public and private acts as your President, I expect to follow my instincts of openness and candor with full confidence that honesty is always the best policy in the end.

My fellow Americans, our long national nightmare is over.

Our Constitution works; our great Republic is a government of laws and not of men. Here the people rule. But there is a higher Power, by whatever name we honor Him, who ordains not only righteousness but love, not only justice but mercy.

As we bind up the internal wounds of Watergate, more painful and more poisonous than those of foreign wars, let us restore the golden rule to our political process, and let brotherly love purge our hearts of suspicion and of hate.

Prayers for Nixon

In the beginning, I asked you to pray for me. Before closing, I ask again your prayers, for Richard Nixon and for his family. May our former President, who brought peace to millions, find it for himself. May God bless and comfort his wonderful wife and daughters, whose love and loyalty will forever be a shining legacy to all who bear the lonely burdens of the White House.

I can only guess at those burdens, although I have witnessed at close hand the tragedies that befell three Presidents and the lesser trials of others.

With all the strength and all the good sense I have gained from life, with all the confidence my family, my friends, and my dedicated staff impart to me, and with the good will of countless Americans I have encountered in recent visits to forty States, I now solemnly reaffirm my promise I made to you last December 6: to uphold the Constitution, to do what is right as God gives me to see the right, and to do the very best I can for America.

God helping me, I will not let you down.

CHAPTER 2

The Watergate
Scandal Unfolds

The Watergate Burglars Are Connected to the White House

Bob Woodward and Carl Bernstein

The Watergate scandal began on June 19, 1972, two days after five men were arrested for burglarizing the Watergate office complex, when the Washington Post *ran a story that for the first time connected one of the burglars to the administration of President Richard M. Nixon. Bob Woodward and Carl Bernstein, the two young* Post *reporters who put together the story, reported that James W. McCord Jr. was a former Central Intelligence Agency (CIA) employee who was working as a paid security coordinator for Nixon's reelection committee—the Committee to Re-elect the President (CRP), later commonly referred to as CREEP. John N. Mitchell, head of the Nixon reelection committee, denied that McCord or the other burglars were operating on the committee's behalf, but this did not prevent the Federal Bureau of Investigation (FBI) from beginning an investigation into the incident. This link of the Watergate burglars to Nixon's administration unleashed an avalanche of investigative journalism by Woodward and Bernstein that made them famous and helped to uncover the truth of the Watergate scandal.*

One of the five men arrested early Saturday [June 17, 1972] in the attempt to bug the Democratic National Committee headquarters is the salaried security coordinator for President Nixon's reelection committee. The suspect, former CIA employee James W. McCord Jr., 53, also holds a separate con-tract to provide security services to the Republican National Committee, GOP ["Grand Old Party," aka, the Republican Party] national chairman Bob Dole said yesterday.

Nixon Reelection Committee Denies Involvement

Former Attorney General John N. Mitchell, head of the Committee for the Re-Election of the President, said yesterday [that] McCord was employed to help install that committee's own security system. In a statement issued in Los Angeles, Mitchell said McCord and the other four men arrested at Democratic headquarters Saturday "were not operating either in our behalf or with our consent" in the alleged bugging attempt.

Dole issued a similar statement, adding that "we deplore action of this kind in or out of politics." An aide to Dole said he was unsure at this time exactly what security services McCord was hired to perform by the National Committee. . . .

Other sources close to the investigation said yesterday that there still was no explanation as to why the five suspects might have attempted to bug Democratic headquarters in the Watergate at 2600 Virginia Ave., NW, or if they were working for other individuals or organizations.

"We're baffled at this point . . . the mystery deepens," a high Democratic party source said. Democratic National Committee Chairman Lawrence F. O'Brien said the "bugging incident . . . raised the ugliest questions about the integrity of the political process that I have encountered in a quarter century. No mere statement of innocence by Mr. Nixon's campaign manager will dispel these questions." The Democratic presidential candidates were not available for comment yesterday.

O'Brien, in his statement, called on Attorney General Richard G. Kleindienst to order an immediate, "searching professional investigation" of the entire matter by the FBI. A spokesman for Kleindienst said yesterday, "The FBI is already investigating. . . . Their investigative report will be turned over to the criminal division for appropriate action." The White House did not comment.

The Five Burglars

McCord, 53, retired from the Central Intelligence Agency in 1970 after 19 years of service and established his own "security consulting firm," McCord Associates, at 414 Hungerford Drive, Rockville [Maryland]. He lives at 7 Winder Ct., Rockville. McCord is an active Baptist and colonel in the Air Force Reserve, according to neighbors and friends.

In addition to McCord, the other four suspects, all Miami residents, have been identified as: Frank Sturgis (also known as Frank Florini), an American who served in Fidel Castro's revolutionary army and later trained a guerrilla force of anti-Castro exiles; Eugenio R. Martinez, a real estate agent and notary public who is active in anti-Castro activities in Miami; Virgilio R. Gonzales, a locksmith; and Bernard L. Barker, a native of Havana said by exiles to have worked on and off for the CIA since the Bay of Pigs invasion in 1961.

All five suspects gave the police false names after being arrested Saturday. McCord also told his attorney that his name is Edward Martin, the attorney said. Sources in Miami said yesterday that at least one of the suspects—Sturgis—was attempting to organize Cubans in Miami to demonstrate at the Democratic National Convention there next month.

The five suspects, well-dressed, wearing rubber surgical gloves and unarmed, were arrested about 2:30 a.m. Saturday when they were surprised by Metropolitan police inside the 29-office suite of the Democratic headquarters on the sixth floor of the Watergate. The suspects had extensive photographic equipment and some electronic surveillance instruments capable of intercepting both regular conversation and telephone communication. Police also said that two ceiling panels near party chairman O'Brien's office had been removed in such a way as to make it possible to slip in a bugging device.

McCord was being held in D.C. jail on $30,000 bond yesterday. The other four were being held there on $50,000 bond. All are charged with attempted burglary and attempted interception of telephone and other conversations.

McCord's Background

McCord was hired as "security coordinator" of the Committee for the Re-election of the President on Jan. 1, according to Powell Moore, the Nixon committee's director of press and information. Moore said McCord's contract called for a "take-home salary of $1,200 per month" and that the ex-CIA employee was assigned an office in the committee's headquarters at 1701 Pennsylvania Ave., N.W. Within the last one or two weeks, Moore said, McCord made a trip to Miami beach—where both the Republican and Democratic National Conventions will be held. The purpose of the trip, Moore said, was "to establish security at the hotel where the Nixon Committee will be staying." In addition to McCord's monthly salary, he and his firm were paid a total of $2,836 by the Nixon Committee for the purchase and rental of television and other security equipment, according to Moore.

Moore said that he did not know exactly who on the committee staff hired McCord, adding that it "definitely wasn't John Mitchell." According to Moore, McCord has never worked in any previous Nixon election campaigns "because he didn't leave the CIA until two years ago, so it would have been impossible." As of late yesterday, Moore said McCord was still on the Re-election Committee payroll.

In his statement from Los Angeles, former Attorney General Mitchell said he was "surprised and dismayed" at reports of McCord's arrest. "The person involved is the proprietor of a private security agency who was employed by our committee months ago to assist with the installation of our security system," said Mitchell. "He has, as we understand it, a number of business clients and interests and we have no knowledge of these relationships." Referring to the alleged attempt to bug the opposition's headquarters, Mitchell said: "There is no place in our campaign, or in the electoral process, for this type of activity and we will not permit it nor condone it."

About two hours after Mitchell issued his statement, GOP National Chairman Dole said, "I understand that Jim McCord . . . is the owner of the firm with which the Republican National Committee contracts for security services . . . if our understanding of the facts is accurate," added Dole, "we will of course discontinue our relationship with the firm." Tom Wilck, deputy chairman of communications for the GOP National Committee, said late yesterday that Republican officials still were checking to find out when McCord was hired, how much he was paid and exactly what his responsibilities were. . . .

After being contacted by *The Washington Post* yesterday, Harlan A. Westrell, who said he was a friend of McCord's, gave the following background on McCord: He is from Texas, where he and his wife graduated from Baylor University. They have three children, a son who is in his third year at the Air Force Academy, and two daughters. The McCords have been active in the First Baptist Church of Washington. Other neighbors said that McCord is a colonel in the Air Force Reserve, and also has taught courses in security at Montgomery Community College. This could not be confirmed yesterday. McCord's previous employment by the CIA was confirmed by the intelligence agency, but a spokesman there said further data about McCord was not available yesterday.

Background on Sturgis and Barker

In Miami, *Washington Post* Staff Writer Kirk Schartenberg reported that two of the other suspects—Sturgis and Barker—are well known among Cuban exiles there. Both are known to have had extensive contracts with the Central Intelligence Agency, exile sources reported, and Barker was closely associated with Frank Bender, the CIA operative who recruited many members of Brigade 2506, the Bay of Pigs invasion force. Barker, 55, and Sturgis, 37, reportedly showed up uninvited at a Cuban exile meeting in May and claimed to represent an anticommunist organization of refugees from "captive nations." The purpose of the meeting, at which both men reportedly spoke, was to plan a Miami demonstration in support of President Nixon's decision to mine the harbor of Haiphong.

Barker, a native of Havana who lived both in the U.S. and Cuba during his youth, is a U.S. Army veteran who was imprisoned in a German POW [prisoner of war] camp during World War II. He later served in the Cuban Buro de Investigationes—secret police—under Fidel Castro and fled to Miami in 1959. He reportedly was one of the principal leaders of the Cuban Revolutionary Council, the exile organization established with CIA help to organize the Bay of Pigs Invasion.

Sturgis, an American soldier of fortune who joined Castro in the hills of Oriente Province in 1958, left Cuba in 1959 with his close friend, Pedro Diaz Lanz, then chief of the Cuban air force. Diaz Lanz, once active in Cuban exile activities in Miami, more recently has been reported involved in such right-wing movements as the John Birch Society and the Rev. Billy James Hargis' Christian Crusade. Sturgis, more commonly known as Frank Florini, lost his American citizenship in 1960 for serving in a foreign military force—Castro's army—but, with the aid of then Florida Sen. George Smathers, regained it.

John Dean's Case Against the President

Time

In May 1973 the Senate Select Committee on Presidential Campaign Activities—often called the Senate Watergate Committee—began hearings on the Watergate break-in and its alleged connection to the president. From June 25 to 29, 1973, the Senate committee, chaired by Senator Sam J. Ervin, heard testimony from White House counsel John Dean. Dean's riveting and nationally televised testimony, given under a grant of immunity from criminal prosecution and described in the following July 9, 1973, article in Time *magazine, broke the investigation wide open because it directly implicated Nixon in the cover-up of the Watergate burglary. Dean testified that Nixon talked to him as early as September 15, 1972, about cover-up activities. Dean said Nixon, on many occasions thereafter, discussed matters such as executive clemency, hush money for the Watergate burglars, and ways to prevent political damage from Justice Department investigations and congressional hearings. Dean also described a climate of fear within the White House that led Nixon staffers to use illegal tactics to undermine political opponents, attack antiwar protesters, punish critics in the press, and collect intelligence on political enemies. Dean's testimony placed even greater political pressure on Nixon as he tried to survive the ensuing scandal.*

Now the grave charges against the President had passed a point of no return. Carried with chilling reality into millions of American homes and spread massively on the official record of a solemn Senate inquiry, the torrential testimony of John W. Dean III fell short of proof in a court of law. But the impact was devastating. As President, Richard Nixon was grievously, if not mortally wounded. . . .

Nixon was a continent away at San Clemente, going about the business of the presidency. He reached a historic compromise with Congress on halting the Cambodia bombing on Aug. 15. He prepared to celebrate the nation's 197th Independence Day, a Fourth of July dimmed by deeply troubling questions (in the words of the Declaration) about the "just powers" of the present Government and by increasing doubts about the "consent of the governed." Though not present in the packed hearing room, Nixon was presonally and directly confronted by the crouched figure of his youthful accuser, until lately his faithful counsel.

Leaning into the microphone, Dean, 34, spoke in a lifeless monotone that would long be remembered by TV audiences. There were just enough unexpected angles and lines in his face, including a slighty crooked grin, to resuce it from mediocrity. Thanks to a pair of glasses, he looked more owlish than his earlier, boyish pictures had suggested.

With impressive poise and masterly memory, Dean spun his detailed web of evidence. He readily admitted his own illegal and improper acts. But he emerged unshaken from five full days of recital and cross-examination, with his basic story challenged but intact.

Clearly, without some kind of direct and detailed Nixon reply, the committee—and the country—would have difficulty believing that the President was not an active and fully aware participant in the Watergate cover-up, as Dean charged. In fact, how and when the President would reply became a decisive factor in his hopes for political survival. Chairman Sam Ervin and other committee members had already begun to ask for his appearance.

With dozens of dates, snatches of dialogue and some documents, Dean had similarly implicated Nixon's most intimate former aides, John Ehrlichman and H.R. [Bob] Haldeman, in multiple actions in the Watergate cover-up. Less vigorously but still deeply, Dean had also drawn into that circle of con-spirators a man he much admires, former Attorney General John Mitchell.

Focusing Blame

While Nixon's deputy press secretary quickly revealed that the President had no intention of submitting himself to senatorial questioning, a White House counterstrategy seemed to be emerging. It was to blame Dean and Mitchell for the Water-gate wiretapping and its concealment. Ehrlichman and Halde-man will likely take the blame for shielding the clandestine ac-tivities of the White House team of agents—"the plumbers"—but plead that these were separate from Watergate and nec-essary in the interests of national security.

The focusing of blame on Mitchell triggered speculation that he might become angry enough to lash back at the entire White House. But his attorney said last week that Mitchell will not implicate the President when he becomes the next Ervin committee witness, as scheduled. Although Mitchell talked al-most daily with Nixon last year even after quitting the President's re-election committee, he has told investigators that nothing the two men discussed would indicate that Nixon knew about the wiretapping in advance or the concealment later or who had been involved. Mitchell will apparently deny, as he has all along, that he never approved the political espio-nage plans.

The White House strategy showed in a harsh assault con-tained in a memo from one of Dean's White House succes-sors, Special Presidential Counsel Fred J. Buzhardt, and a list of 39 White House-inspired questions. Read by Senator Daniel Inouye, they failed to rattle the accuser. Contradicting point after point in quick response, Dean easily handled the attack.

Indeed, the effort backfired, which is perhaps why the White House quickly disavowed it and said that it was merely Lawyer Buzhardt's friendly personal contribution on the proceedings. It failed by straining credulity in portraying the slender, subservient Dean, a born follower, as the "mastermind" in the Watergate cover-up, with former Attorney General John Mitchell as "his patron." It contended, in effect, that this cunning pair participated in planning the political espionage at Democratic National Headquarters and then, to conceal that fact, they hindered the investigation by the FBI, compromised the CIA, ordered evidence shredded, and arranged for payoffs and offers of Executive clemency to the arrested burglars to ensure their silence. Creating a constitutional crisis almost alone, the Buzhardt statement in effect charged, Dean and Mitchell kept the truth of all that concealed for some nine months from such shrewd White House officials as H.R. Haldeman, John Ehrlichman, Charles W. Colson—and the President.

While White House records and future witnesses before Senator Sam Ervin's Watergate committee may yet impugn Dean's story in a convincing way, it emerged from last week's test by fire as more credible than either Buzhardt's conspiracy theory or the President's less accusatory brief of last May 22. Instead of depicting a duped President and innocent top-level aides, Dean's damning version held that the lawless efforts to conceal the political implications of Watergate were an automatic and widespread White House response intended to protect the President's re-election prospects—and Nixon as a self-interested participant. Dean admitted his own role, but said that, rather than being what Buzhardt termed "the principal actor," he took orders, often reluctantly, from his domineering superiors, Haldeman and Ehrlichman. Claiming relatively little influence in shaping policy at the White House, Dean insisted that "my title was the best part of the job."

More specifically, Dean contended that the Watergate wiretapping operation was known in the White House by Chief of Staff Haldeman before the June 17 arrests—and since Haldeman regularly reported fully to the President, Dean "assumed"

Nixon could have known. He said that he did not know first-hand, however, whether Nixon did, in fact, have such advance knowledge.

But, as early as Sept. 15, Dean charged, the President clearly indicated his awareness that a cover-up was under way. Then and later, Dean claimed, the President talked directly to him about Executive clemency and hush money for the wiretappers, as well as about ways to prevent the potential damage of Justice Department investigations, Democratic Party civil suits and congressional hearings.

If Dean's claims are true—and his supporting details as well as some of his circumstantial documents were impressive—that would make Nixon's May 22 denials outright lies or at least render the presidential statements once again "inoperative." At that time Nixon said flatly that he had known nothing about offers of clemency or of any efforts to provide the defendants with funds and that he had taken no part in any efforts to cover up Watergate.

Dean's direct charges against the President still lacked corroboration. Dean's motives remained suspect, since he obviously hoped to avoid a long prison term for his admitted illegal acts. Yet even if those facts leave many unconvinced of Nixon's complicity in Watergate, Dean's dismaying description of the climate of fear existing within the Nixon White House is almost as alarming as the affair that it spawned. With little regard for the law and under repeated proddings by the President himself, Dean contended, the Nixon staff used or contemplated using almost any available tactic to undermine political opponents, punish press critics, subdue antiwar protesters and gather political intelligence, including lists of "enemies."

Dean insisted that in this fortress of fear he served "as a restraining influence against many wild and crazy schemes." Periodic surveillance of Senator Edward Kennedy was surreptitiously ordered, even when he was on a trip to India, but it turned up nothing of interest to the White House. However, when a round-the-clock tailing of Kennedy was demanded by Haldeman, Dean got the project canceled on the sound theory that the tracker might be mistaken for somone posing a threat to Kennedy's life.

Although a Colson associate later claimed that it was only a joke, Dean took seriously Colson's suggestion that Washington's Brookings Institution be fire-bombed and raided to get some politically sensitive papers. In fact, Dean grabbed a military jet to California in order to persuade Ehrlichman to order Colson to forget the idea. Dean said he simply filed away many suggestions that he considered extreme and responded to them only if there were persistent pressures from his superiors.

It was Nixon's personal outrage at being exposed to demonstrators that seemed most dramatically to set the pre-Watergate White House mood. Dean told of Nixon's spotting "a lone man with a large ten-foot sign stretched out in front of Lafayette Park" within sight of his window. Soon a White House aide was rushing to round up "thugs" to take care of the protester. Dean intervened, got police to persuade the man to move. A man who broke police lines during Nixon's Inauguration but was knocked down by Secret Service agents well short of Nixon's car so angered the President that Dean was repeatedly badgered for not getting the man prosecuted. An investigation was launched, but Dean found that the trespasser had had no intention of harming the President. Dean could only explain helplessly that crossing a police barricade was too trifling a violation for officals to pursue.

However trivial each of such incidents seemed in isolation, together they formed an ominous pattern that made Watergate comprehensible to Dean. What he called "an isatiable appetite for political intelligence" stemmed directly from Nixon, as Dean told it in his matter-of-fact manner. The President was convinced that antiwar Senators had links with U.S. radicals, who had foreign ties, and he continually demanded evidence of this. Intelligence agencies repeatedly said it was not necessarily so. "We never found a scintilla of evidence . . . this was explained to Mr. Haldeman, but the President believed that the opposite was, in fact, true." He demanded better intelligence.

Lawyer-like, Dean resisted most attempts by the committee to draw him into discussing personalities or making value judgments. He conceded that the Watergate break-in was "the first act in a great American tragedy" and said he found it "very difficult" to testify about what others, including "men I greatly admire and respect," had done. He found it easier to admit that he had obstructed justice and helped another man commit perjury in the affair. Yet Dean's story did, indeed, indict others.

How It Began

Dean reported having attended two meetings in Attorney General Mitchell's office on Jan. 27 and Feb. 4, 1972, at which G. Gordon Liddy, counsel for the Nixon re-election committee, presented his bizarre intelligence-gathering plans. Dean's testimony generally agreed with that of Jeb Stuart Magruder, the Nixon committee's deputy director, who had also been present at the two meetings. Dean added some refinements: Liddy's first proposals included the use of "mugging squads" to rough up demonstrators, and the employment of prostitutes—"high class and the best in the business"—to entice secrets out of Democrats at Miami Beach.

Mitchell, said Dean, "was amazed. I gave him a look of bewilderment and he winked. He took a few long puffs on his pipe and told Liddy that the plan he had developed was not quite what he had in mind and the cost [$1,000,000] was out of the question." Dean arrived late for the second meeting, discovered Liddy was still discussing illegal wiretapping plans, objected that "these discussions could not go in the office of the Attorney General," and cut the meeting short; "terminated" it, to use Dean's invariable terminology. Dean thought the plans were dead.

Magruder testified that a scaled-down espionage plan had later been reluctantly approved by Mitchell at a third meeting in Key Biscayne on March 30. Dean, who had not attended that meeting, said he still did not know if the plan had actually been approved. Also present was Frederick LaRue, an aide to Mitchell after the latter shifted to head the Nixon campaign; he has said his boss did not approve. LaRue pleaded guilty last week to one count of obstruction of justice—the first high-level Nixonite to do so—and he will apparently become a Government witness against others. Testified Dean: "I do not know to this day who kept pushing for these plans— whether Liddy was pushing or whether Magruder was pushing or whether someone was pushing Magruder."

How The Cover-up Spread

The cover-up began, said Dean, the moment it was learned that James McCord, security chief for the Nixon committee, was one of the men arrested at the Watergate on June 17 and that one of the other burglars carried a check from E. Howard Hunt Jr., a White House consultant. Apparently the first destruction of evidence was done by Gordon Strachan, who had served as liaison between the Nixon committee and Haldeman. Dean said that, on Haldeman's oders, Strachan had destroyed files from Haldeman's office, including "wiretap information from the D.N.C." (Democratic National Committee). Dean said he was then told by Ehrlichman to get word to Hunt "to get out of the country." Dean did so, but later the two reconsidered, though it unwise, and tried to rescind the order.

Since Magruder had testified that he had passed along wiretapping plants and transcripts of some of the illegal interceptions to Strachan on the assumption that they would go to

Haldeman, this destruction of records seems to confirm that they had reached Haldeman. Strachan, who has been offered limited immunity by the Ervin committee, thus apparently could discredit Haldeman's adamant denials of any advance knowledge of the Watergate wiretapping.

Ehrlichman's orders to get Hunt out of the country similarly implicate Nixon's other intimate aide in the first moments of the concealment. If both Haldeman and Ehrlichman lose credibility, the President's denials of cover-up knowledge would apparently have to rest on the claim that all of his close aides had deceived him, not just Dean and Mitchell.

Ehrlichman's Role

Dean related another significant attempt to destroy evidence, this one originating with Ehrlichman. Dean had been given custody of the material found in the safe of Hunt, who had been employed as one of the news-leak-plugging White House "plumbers." Among the contents were a briefcase containing "loose wires, Chap Sticks with wires coming out of them, and instruction sheets for walkie-talkies." The papers included a fake State Department cable linking the Kennedy Administration to the 1963 assassination of South Viet Nam's President Diem and a psychological profile of former Pentagon Papers Defendant Daniel Ellsberg. Dean considered these "political dynamite." He asked Ehrlichman what to do with them.

"He told me to shred the documents and 'deep-six' the briefcase. I asked him what he meant by deep-six. He leaned back in his chair and said: 'You drive across the river on your way home at night, don't you? Well, when you cross over the bridge on your way home, just toss the briefcase into the river.' I told him in a joking manner that I would bring the materials over to him and he could take care of them because he also crossed the river on his way home. He said no thank you." Ehrlichman, asked about this by [Television Commentator] Mike Wallace on CBS's *60 Minutes*, replied that "shredding is an activity that has been foreign to my nature. I don't think I have shredded or requested the shredding of a document since I came to Washington five years ago."

Gray's Participation

Dean said he thought it would be "incredible" to destroy evidence and finally decided not to follow Ehrlichman's orders. Instead, the political documents were given by Dean and Ehrlichman to then Acting FBI Director L. Patrick Gray III, with the warning that they must "never be leaked or made public." Gray later admitted destroying them, claiming he thought he had been told to do so by Ehrlichman and Dean. That admission led to Gray's prompt resignation as acting director— although his failure to win Senate confirmation had made his departure a certainty anway.

Enter Mardian

In a move that Dean said was first suggested by Robert Mardian, former head of the Justice Department's Internal Security Division, and approved by both Mitchell and Ehrlichman, Dean tried to get CIA help in impeding the FBI's investigation in Mexico of campaign money that had financed the Watergate wiretapping. The White House hoped that the CIA could also provide covert payments to the restive defendants. Ehrlichman told Dean to work through Deputy CIA Director Vernon Walters rather than Director Richard Helms because "the White House had put him [Walters] in the deputy-director position so they could have some influence over the agency." After some hesitation, Walters proved to be unhelpful, thereby angering Ehrlichman.

Enlisting Kalmbach

The need for hush money was growing more urgent, and Dean was told by Mitchell to get Haldeman and Ehrlichman to approve the use of President Nixon's personal lawyer, Herbert Kalmbach, in helping raise the money. Dean said the two presidential aides agreed and Kalmbach unhappily accepted the assignment. He was told by Dean to ask LaRue for details on how much to pay each of the wiretappers and to make his own arrangements for delivering the cash. Kalmbach later reported that he had performed this job. The payments of silence money thus became one of the most specific and widespread obstructions of justice, involving at that time at least Dean, Mitchell, Haldeman, Ehrlichman, Kalmbach and LaRue—if Dean's account is true.

The Dean "Report"

Dean first became publicly linked with the President's defense on Watergate when, to his "great surprise," he heard Nixon announce on Aug. 29 that a report by Dean had cleared everyone then employed at the White House of any Watergate involvement. Dean insisted he had never made either an investigation or a report and, if he had been asked, would have "strongly opposed the issuing of such a statement" because he thought it was untrue. It could only be true if it was narrowly construed to mean actual knowledge of the June 17 break-in since, Dean still believes, only the wiretapping team knew that its second break-in, to repair malfunctioning equipment, was to be made on that date. For the first time, Dean began to wonder if he was being "set up in case the whole thing came crumbling down at a later time."

The La Costa Meetings

Wary of the impending Ervin hearings, Haldeman, Ehrlichman, Dean and Nixon Aide Richard Moore met at La Costa Resort Hotel near San Clemente in February to plan how to deal with this newest threat to the cover-up. The group was puzzled about who would be friend and who would be foe on the Senate committee. Ehrlichman quipped that the name of Hawaii's Democratic Senator Daniel Inouye should be pronounced "ain't-no-way" because "there ain't no way he's going to give us anything but problems." Senator Lowell Weiker, according to Dean, "was an independent who could give the White House problems"; neither Haldeman nor Ehrlichman knew "which way Senator [Howard] Baker might go." To the White House staff, the only certain bet was Florida's Republican Senator Edward J. Gurney, who was described as "a sure friend and protector of the President's interests."

A decision was made at La Costa, Dean said, to profess cooperation with the committee but privately attempt "to restrain the investigation and make it as difficult as possible to get information and witnesses." The group discuessed means of trying to prove that Democrats had undertaken Watergate-like snooping and bugging in their campaigns. Incredibly, Haldeman suggested that the Nixon re-election committee might "hire private investigators to dig out information on the Democrats." Dean objected on grounds that "this would be more political surveillance—yet the matter was left unresolved."

But it was the critical contacts between Dean and the President that go to the core of the momentous controversy. Confirming a Dean claim that it had at first sharply denied, the White House last week agreed that there had been at least 22 meetings and 14 telephone conversations between the two men. The sudden increase in the frequency of communication led Dean to wonder whether Nixon might be creating a basis for claiming Executive privilege and an attorney-client relationship in order to protect himself. Dean's version of the most significant of the meetings:

Sept. 15, 1972

The Watergate grand jury in Washington had just handed down its indictments, which reached no higher than the Nixon finance committee's counsel, [G. Gordon] Liddy. Summoned to the Oval Office in the late afternoon, Dean found the President and Haldeman "in very good spirits, and my reception was very warm and cordial." Then, in Dean's damning recollection, "the President told me that Bob had kept him posted on my handling of the Watergate case. The President told me I had done a good job and he appreciated how difficult a task it had been and the President was pleased that the case had stopped with Liddy."

Reinforcing the point that there could be no misunderstanding of why the President was congratulating him, Dean testified: "I responded that I could not take credit because others had done much more difficult things than I had done." (Dean later explained to the Ervin committee that he was thinking of [Nixon committee deputy director Jeb] Magruder, for one, who had perjured himself, after coaching from Dean, to keep the grand jury from learning of higher involvement.) "I also told him that there was a long way to go before this matter would end, and that I certainly could make no assurance that the day would not come when this matter would start to unravel." Dean told the President that there would be a good chance to delay the Democratic civil suits against the Nixon committee until after the election because committee lawyers were talking out of court to the judge, Charles R. Richey, who was "very understanding and trying to accommodate their problems." Said Nixon: "Well, that's helpful." Richey dismissed Dean's story as "poppycock."

If accurate, Dean's account meant that the President was encouraging the cover-up in the criminal case and was approving attempts to influence the judge in the civil suits.

Later, Senator [Edward] Gurney sharply probed Dean's contention that Nixon was unmistakably congratulating him for limiting the Watergate indictments. Asked Gurney: "How can you say that the President knew all about these things from a simple observation by him that 'Bob tells me you are doing a good job'?" This led Dean to shift slightly his version of the President's wording and then complain: "We are quibbling over words." Snapped Gurney: "We are talking about something very important, whether the President of the United States knew on Sept. 15 about the Watergate and the cover-up." Then the Senator summed up: "Your whole theory on saying that the President of the United States knew about Watergate on Sept. 15 is purely an impression; there isn't a single shred of evidence that came out of this meeting."

Feb. 27, 1973

The President told Dean that the Watergate affair was taking up too much of the time of his two top assistants, Haldeman and Ehrlichman, and therefore Dean could stop reporting through them and deal directly with him. Nixon gave another puzzling reason: "He also told me that they were principals in the matter and I, therefore, could be more objective than they." Dean said he was not sure later what the President had meant by calling them "principals."

Nixon, Dean testified, also told him that he "would never let Haldeman and Ehrlichman go to the Hill" to appear at the Ervin committee hearings. He would protect them with a claim of Executive privilege and would, at most, permit his aides to respond to written questions. Dean agreed that these "could be handled."

Feb. 28, 1973

Dean made his first attempt to warn Nixon of the seriousness of the affair from a legal standpoint. "I told him that I thought he should know that I was also involved in the post-June 17 activities regarding Watergate. I briefly described to him why I thought I had legal problems in that I had been a conduit for many of the decisions that were made and therefore could be involved in an obstruction of justice. He would not accept my analysis and did not want me to get into it in any detail."

The President had thus been told by his counsel that the cover-up might have involved crimes, but he chose for unexplained reasons to brush this aside. Despite a public posture of seeking to get out the truth, he was privately working, by Dean's account, against full disclosure to the Ervin committee. A White House version of this meeting sharply contradicts Dean. It says he assured Nixon that there was no White House involvement.

March 13, 1973

For the first time, Dean said, he talked directly to the President about the payment of hush money to the seven Watergate defendants. When Haldeman was in the room, Dean related, "I told the President that there was no money to pay these individuals to meet their demands. He asked me how much it would cost. I told him that I could only estimate, that it might be as high as a million dollars or more. He told me that that was no problem and he also looked over at Haldeman and repeated the statement. He then asked me who was demanding this money, and I told him it was principally coming from Hunt through his attorney."

Dean said: "The President then referred to the fact that Hunt had been promised Executive clemency. He said that he had discussed this matter with Ehrlichman and, contrary to instructions that Ehrlichman had given [White House counsel Charles] Colson not to talk to the President about it, that Colson had also discussed it with him later. He expressed some annoyance at this."

Nixon has denied authorizing or knowing anything about these two elements in the cover-up—promises of Executive clemency and payoffs to keep the conspirators quiet—both of which could be considered obstruction of justice. The White House offered a totally different version of the discussion of the $1,000,000. Nixon was said to have dismissed such payments as "blackmail" and scoffed at paying it. Also, the White House claimed that this topic came up on March 21 rather than [on] this date.

March 21, 1973 (Morning)

Still hoping that Nixon would order all concealment efforts ended and the truth revealed, Dean said, he put the matter as dramatically as he could. "I began by telling the President that there was a cancer growing on the presidency and that if the cancer was not removed, that the President himself would be killed by it. I also told him that it was important that this cancer be removed immediately because it was growing more deadly every day."

Dean then laid out the whole story, noting the two Liddy-Mitchell-Magruder meetings he had attended before the wire-tapping and adding that he had reported these plans to Haldeman. He said that both Haldeman and Mitchell had received wiretap information. After June 17, he reported, [Nixon's personal lawyer Herbert] Kalmbach had paid silence money on instructions relayed by Dean from Ehrlichman, Haldeman and Mitchell. Dean said that he had helped prepare Magruder for perjured testimony. "I concluded by saying that it is going to take continued perjury and continued support of these individuals to perpetuate the cover-up and that I did not believe that it was possible to so continue it. Rather, all those involved must stand up and account for themselves and the President himself must get out in front."

But, said Dean, Nixon did not seem to understand, and set up a meeting of Haldeman, Ehrlichman, Mitchell and Dean. The hope was that Mitchell would take the blame for the Watergate wiretapping and that the public would then be satisfied and stop the clamor over the cover-up. (At the meeting the next day, Mitchell made no effort to do this, and nothing was decided.)

March 21, 1973 (Afternoon)

At a second meeting with the President, Haldeman and Ehrlichman provided another "tremendous disappointment" for Dean. "It was quite clear that the cover-up as far as the White

House was concerned was going to continue." Dean said he thought Haideman and Ehrlichman as well as himself were indictable for obstruction of justice and that "it was time that everybody start thinking about telling the truth." Dean said Haldeman and Ehrlichman "were very unhappy with my comments."

Thus the President, said Dean, had been extensively briefed on the legal implications but took no action to alter the way in which the situation was being handled. The White House version claims that a tentative decision was reached that everyone go to the grand jury, but Dean wanted immunity.

Feeling increasingly isolated, Dean was invited by the President to take his wife Maureen to Camp David for a rest. When he arrived, Haldeman was calling and asked for a full report on Watergate. Dean began writing his report. New problems lay ahead, however, as Wiretapper James McCord had written his letter to Judge [John] Sirica charging that others were involved in Watergate. Newsmen were probing anew, another grand jury session seemed likely, and the Ervin hearings were growing closer. Dean called a lawyer for advice, came down from the mountain, found what he felt was a new and "back-pedaling" Haldeman. "He was beginning to protect his flanks." Dean decided not to turn over his report but to seek more legal advice and begin a series of secret meetings with the Justice Department prosecutors. He withheld his decision from everyone at the White House.

On April 8 Dean decided to tell Haldeman that be was going to talk to the prosecutors. Haldeman advised against it, saying: "Once the toothpaste is out of the tube, it's going to be very hard to get it back in." Dean compiled a list of 15 names of those he thought indictable; out of the 15 persons noted, ten were lawyers. He showed it to Ehrlichman—and soon got word from the prosecutors saying that further secret talks were off. The President wanted a full report from Attorney General Richard Kleindienst on the progress of the Watergate investigation.

April 15, 1973

Once again, Dean requested a meeting with Nixon. The thrust of the President's questions led Dean to think the conversation was being taped. Nixon said "he had, of course, only been joking" about his earlier reference to $1,000,000 for silence, and he told Dean that any conversations with him were privileged or covered by national security or both. But the most interesting moment, Dean said, was when Nixon "went behind his chair to the corner of the office and in a nearly inaudible tone said to me he was probably foolish to have discussed Hunt's clemency with Colson." The conversation ended with Dean saying he hoped nothing he did would "result in the impeachment of the President." Nixon replied joking: "I certainly hope so also." The White House report contends that Nixon told Dean he must go before the grand jury without immunity.

April 16, 1973

Nixon summoned Dean to his office, handed him two terse letters, and asked him to sign either one. One said that Dean was resigning "as a result of my involvement in the Watergate matter"; the other gave as the cause "my increasing involvement in the Watergate matter." Dean refused to sign unless Ehrlichman and Haldeman would sign the same letter. Nixon said that Dean could draft his own letter, and Dean did so, trying to request for a leave of absence to similar moves by the other two aides. Unhappily, Nixon said "it wasn't what he wanted." On April 30, Nixon announced on television that he had fired Dean and accepted the resignation of Ehrlichman and Haldeman, praising them as "two of the finest public servants it has been my privilege to know."

Through four further days of questioning, sometimes gentle but others jarring, Dean stuck stubbornly to that basic story. To support it, he submitted more than 50 documents to the committee. These ranged from memos on the illegal 1970 domestic-security plans approved for a time by the President, to a paper on how the White House could leak a news story on why the leaking of Government secrets is bad. Dean seemed to falter only under the persistent and skillful grilling of Senator Gurney.

Gurney bore into Dean's admitted personal use of $4,850 in campaign money that was being kept in his office safe. Dean insisted he had deposited a check for that amount to cover it. Gurney produced a Dean bank-account statement showing that the check was not good at the time it was placed in the safe and said Dean could be guilty of embezzlement. Dean's lawyer sharply objected to that interpretation of law, and Dean said he had never had any intention not to repay the money. He was later partly rescued by Senator Sam Ervin, who introduced a brokerage-account statement showing that Dean had more than $26,000 available at the time. Yet Dean's explanation that he took the cash for his honeymoon and other expenses rather than use credit cards seemed lame.

Gurney also surprised Dean on a minor confusion about the hotel in which he had discussed hush funds with Nixon's attorney Kalmbach. Was it Washington's Mayflower Hotel, as he had testified, even though Kalmbach had been registered on that date at the Statler Hilton? After some sparring, Dean, prompted by his lawyer, said that he often confused the two and could have been mistaken, since the Statler Hilton's coffee shop is called the Mayflower.

Questions For Dean

The main thrust of the critical questioning of Dean was along several lines:

Had not Dean and his lawyers waged a campaign to gain him immunity from criminal prosecution, in part by using news leaks that exaggerate the importance of what he might know? Dean was not entirely convincing in saying that he had no idea how some of his testimony had got into news reports before his appearance, but his testimony last week was a sure demonstration that he did indeed have vast and impressive knowledge of the whole conspiracy.

If Dean was so concerned about the cover-up activity, why, as the President's counsel, did he not warn Nixon long before he did? Dean claimed that his reporting channels were through Haldeman or Ehrlichman and that, despite his title, he could not barge into the President's office. Moreover he assumed that his superiors would keep the President fully informed of his reports on a matter as vital as Watergate.

If he considered his meetings with the President so significant, why did he not keep precise written records on the converstaions? Dean's answer was reasonable: "I thought they were very incriminating to the President of the United States."

Questions For Nixon

A bewildering array of specific questions for the President is suggested in each of Dean's charges and interpretations of conversations between them. So far, the President's press spokesmen have responded only by saying that Nixon will stand behind his May 22 statement. That consisted of making blanket denials rather than dealing with specific meetings and events. Nixon, for example, claimed that he had had no knowledge of the White House–ordered burglary of Daniel Ellsberg's psychiatrist's office until he made an investigation late in March of 1973. Yet Dean testified that one of the plumber team's leaders, Egil Krogh, told him that orders for the break-in had come "right out of the Oval Office." Even a White House–provided log of conversations with Dean indicates that Nixon was told about the burglary more than a month before the judge in the case was notified by the Administration. The Ellsberg "bag job" was similar to the illegal activities authorized under an intelligence plan that Nixon admits had his approval briefly in 1970. Dean said that as White House counsel, he never saw firm evidence that the plan had, in fact, been rescinded.

But the more significant queries for Nixon raised by the Dean testimony are these: Did he discuss Executive clemecy with Ehrlichman and Colson, as Dean claims? Did he congratulate Dean on helping to limit the Watergate indictments? Did he scoff at the $1,000,000 in payoff money, as the White House claims? Is there a tape, as Dean suspected, of the meeting in which Nixon claimed to have been joking about the $1,000,000 in silence money?

The two most accusatory summations were drawn by Lowell Weicker and Sam Ervin. Weicker, clearly outraged at what he considered continuing Nixon Administration connivance in trying to "grossly" subvert its political foes, including himself, erupted in the week's most impassioned oratory. Scathingly, he launched into a litany of what he called "proven or admitted" crimes committed by the Executive Branch of the Government.

The list was long: conspiracy to obstruct justice, conspiracy to intercept wire or oral communications, subornation of perjury, conspiracy to obstruct a criminal investigation, conspiracy to destroy evidence, conspiracy to file false sworn statements, conspiracy to commit breaking and entering, conspiracy to commit burglary, misprision of a felony, filing of false sworn statements, perjury, breaking and entering, burglary, interception of wire and oral communications, obstruction of criminal investigation, attempted interference with administration of the Internal Revenue laws, and attempted unauthorized use of Internal Revenue information.

Chairman Ervin built a virtual case of impeachment against the President by leading Dean through a series of questions on Ervin's most revered topic, the U.S. Constitution. "And I will ask you as a lawyer if you do not think that surreptitious entry or burglary and electronic surveillance and penetration constituted a violation of the Fourth Amendment?"

Dean: Yes sir, I do.

Ervin noted the name of Sam M. Lambert, former executive secretary of the National Education Association, on a White House "enemy" list because he opposed federal aid to parochial schools. "Here is a man listed among the opponents whose only offense is that he believed in the First Amendment and shared Thomas Jefferson's conviction, as expressed in the Virginia Statute for Religious Freedom, that to compel a man to make contributions of money for dissemination of religious opinions he disbelieves is sinful and tyrannical. Isn't that true?"

Dean: I cannot disagree with the chairman at all.

Ervin: Article II of the Constitution says in defining the power of the President, Section 3 of Article II—"He"—that is, the President—"shall take care that the laws be faithfully executed." Do you know anything that the President did or said at any time between June 17 and the present moment to perform his duty to see that the laws are faithfully executed in respect to what is called the Watergate affair?

Dean: I have given the facts as I know them and I don't . . . I would rather be excused from drawing my own conclusion on that at this point in time.

Ervin declared pointedly that in "the experience of the English-speaking race" the only reliable way of testing the credibility of a witness is through interrogation. The committee almost certainly cannot compel Nixon to testify, the constitutional issue of whether a President can be subpoenaed being murky. But Senator Baker pointed out that Woodrow Wilson, rather than appear before a congressional committee, invited the committee to meet him, and Weicker recalled that a senate committee during the Civil War had decided to investigate whether Mary Todd Lincoln was a "disloyalist." Then Weicker read from Carl Sandburg's moving account of how that earlier committee's chairman perceived the episode.

"At the foot of the committee table, solitary, his hat in his hand, Abraham Lincoln stood. . . . The President had not been asked to come before the committee, nor was it suspected that he had information that we were to investigate reports, which, if true, fastened treason upon his family in the White House. As last, the mourning corpus spoke, slowly, with a depth of sorrow in his voice: 'I, Abraham Lincoln, President of the United States, appear of my own volition before this committee of the Senate to say that I, of my own knowledge, know that it is untrue that any of my family hold treasonable communication with the enemy.'"

"Having attested this, he went away as silent and solitary as he had come. We sat for some moments speechless and, by tacit agreement, no word being spoken, the committee dropped all consideration of the rumors."

It remains to be seen whether Richard Nixon will elect to emulate the first Republican President and come before the Ervin committee, "solitary, his hat in his hand," to answer the charges about Watergate. It would certainly require more than a simple, solemn declaration of his innocence. The scene is difficult to imagine, to be sure, but in the end it may become the only way to restore any degree of public trust in his presidency.

Hearts and Flowers from John Dean

It had been an extraordinary physical and emotional ordeal for John Dean. Most evenings after the hearings, he and his two attorneys, Robert McCandless and Charles Shaffer, retreated to Dean's town house in Alexandria, Va. There, Maureen, his brittlely attractive wife who sat somewhat tensely behind Dean in the hearing room, prepared hamburgers. Then Dean and the lawyers went over the day's testimony and watched evening newscasts but not reruns of the day's performance. After a hot bath and a rubdown by "Mo," Dean would get to sleep by 11:30 p.m. Despite the tension, he said he slept well.

Shortly after the last session, Dean sank into an easy chair, Maureen near him. He agreed to discuss the personal aspects of his week that was with TIME Correspondent Hays Gorey, who had followed him to his home. The cool, meticulous and rather scholarly-looking Dean of the hearings seemed to fade away, as did (at least in his own mind) the earlier Dean, deeply involved in the illegal and unsavory acts. A third Dean emerged, still pleading his case but giving a strangely sentimental picture of his life.

What had been the most difficult aspect of the week of testimony?

Physically, the most exhausting thing was to read my opening statement. Emotionally, the most difficult aspects were having to talk about the President of the United States as the truth demanded and having to involve former associates and friends.

What sustained him during the week?

I knew what I knew. I had no fear of being tripped up in cross-examination. Really, to tell the truth is the easiest thing in the world.

Did he think he was bringing down the Republic or restoring it?

There's a cloud over this city. Until this cloud is removed, the Government will not operate. This nation will recover only when we get to the bottom of this situation. I look upon myself as one who is helping the process.

What thoughts had been running through his mind?

Let me tell you a story. When I was five or six or seven, I was playing with matches behind the garage. There was lots of brush there. It caught fire and burned down the back of the garage. My father asked me if I had done it. I said no. But of course my father knew I had done it. He sent me to my room, saying "John, we'll talk again when you are ready to tell the truth." Then he did a wise thing. While I was in my room, he sent the fire marshal to talk to me. He must have been ten feet tall, wearing a big blue uniform. I can see him to this day. He said to me: "Now, John, you haven't told your father the truth." The impact of the blue uniform as the authority of the law was enormous. I said to myself: "The jig is up." I told my father. He said: "The best way is—tell the truth."

The truth emerges. There's no doubt about it. I expressed the hope today that the Ervin hearings will bring out all the truth, but even if they do not, some day all these facts will come out.

What had he relied upon during the ordeal?

Prayers. Every night, the last thing we do before going to sleep, Mo and I ask each other, "Did you say your prayers?" I almost went into the Episcopal ministry, you know. And I want to tell you, the love of this woman has been one of the greatest sources of strength. You can't imagine how great.

But how had he got involved in the Watergate mess?

Well, one reason, I suppose, is that I have always been ambitious, always wanted to get ahead. I remember an uncle of mine who once cautioned me: "John, you've got to stop to smell the flowers."

Why had he participated in the cover-up for so long?

Here's an analogy that may make it more understandable. I watch crew racing quite often out there on the Potomac River. You know, if you get involved in crew racing, you're on the team. I pulled my oar a long time. Suddenly I realized the race was over, and that we were going to wrong way. But you know what happens when you drop your oar? It may throw you out of the boat. Well, finally I did drop my oar, and I've been trying to swim to shore ever since—through a lot of muck.

Did he have any regrets?

I should say not. Life is much easier when you can be open. Back to the crew-race analogy again, I did try for a long time to tell the coxswain that the race was over and that we were rowing in the wrong direction. But he wasn't listening, and a couple of members of the crew were still rowing.

What about the future?

I really haven't given that a lot of thought. Some, but not a lot. I do know this: I'm grateful that I am young enough to have plenty of time now to stop and smell the flowers. There are many things I enjoy doing that I haven't given myself time to do. Now I will. I did, after all, rise to a very high position in the Government. I've been there, and I have no desire to go back.

The Saturday Night Massacre

Alexander Burns

In 1973 President Richard Nixon repeatedly refused to hand over secret presidential tape recordings to Archibald Cox, the special prosecutor investigating the Watergate break-in. In the fall of that year, Nixon tried to negotiate for an edited release of some of the taped information, but Cox rejected the compromise and planned to appeal the matter to the U.S. Supreme Court. Before Cox could appeal, Nixon on October 20, 1973, ordered Attorney General Elliot Richardson to fire Cox. Both Richardson and Deputy Attorney General William D. Ruckelshaus, however, refused to do so and resigned. Finally, Solicitor General Robert H. Bork, who became acting attorney general after Ruckelshaus's discharge, dismissed Cox. Nixon's decision to fire Cox set off a wave of protests and a flood of letters to Congress and the White House. As Harvard University scholar Alexander Burns explains in the following October 20, 2005, article posted at the American Heritage *Web site, the whole affair, dubbed the "Saturday Night Massacre," marked the beginning of the end of Nixon's presidency.*

On the night of Saturday, October 20, 1973, . . . the Watergate special prosecutor, Archibald Cox, received a chilling message. He knew the message was coming, and he knew what it would say, but that didn't dull the shock of it. President Richard M. Nixon had had the attorney general of the United States fire him. Attorney General Elliot Richardson had refused to do it, and had been forced to resign; Deputy Attorney General William Ruckelshaus had then also refused and also resigned; finally, Solicitor General Robert Bork—who would later be nominated, unsuccessfully, to the Supreme Court—assumed the post of acting head of the Justice De-

Alexander Burns, "October 20, 1973: Massacre at the White House," americanheritage. com, October 20, 2005. Reprinted by permission of American Heritage Inc.

partment and carried out the President's order. The serial firings of that October evening quickly became known as the Saturday Night Massacre. They represented both a profound challenge to the American justice system and a turning point in the downfall of Richard Nixon.

The Climax of the Watergate Drama

The Saturday Night Massacre was a climax in a drama that had been unfolding for more than a year. On June 17, 1972, five men had been caught breaking into the Democratic National Committee's offices in Washington's Watergate office-apartment complex. As evidence slowly emerged tying the President's close associates to the crime, Congress launched an investigation into the incident and subsequent cover-up. After this led to the resignation of three top Nixon officials—White House Chief of Staff H.R. Haldeman, chief domestic policy adviser John Ehrlichman, and Attorney General Richard Kleindienst—the Justice Department appointed Archibald Cox to the position of special prosecutor, to make possible a fair and impartial investigation of the whole matter. Then, during July 1973, a Nixon aide named Alexander Butterfield told the Senate committee investigating Watergate that the President kept a voice-activated tape recorder in the Oval Office. Both Congress and the special prosecutor jumped on this revelation and launched efforts to obtain all the tape recordings that had been made. With that information, they hoped, they could finally answer Tennessee Senator Howard Baker's famous question: "What did the President know and when did he know it?"

Nixon and his allies resisted these efforts furiously, but on October 12, 1973, the U.S. Circuit Court of Appeals for the District of Columbia ordered the White House to comply with Cox's subpoena demanding the full collection of tapes. In the following week the Nixon administration attempted to negotiate a deal with Cox whereby Democratic Senator John

Stennis of Mississippi would listen to the tapes and write summaries of them for Cox. Nixon's deal, an obvious attempt to circumvent the appeals court's ruling, was unacceptable to the prosecutor, and he said as much in a press conference on October 19. By rejecting Nixon's proposal, Cox provided the President with a pretext for a drastic measure of self-defense: firing the investigator. Choosing Saturday as this moment of action because of the traditional lack of news coverage that night, Nixon launched a series of events that would spark broad public outcry and accelerate his already quickening decline.

In the aftermath of the Saturday Night Massacre and the announcement that the White House was abolishing the Office of the Special Watergate Prosecutor, public indignation was so intense that Nixon almost immediately had to backtrack. Millions expressed outrage in telegrams, phone calls, and letters. On November 1 the new White House chief of staff, future Presidential candidate Gen. Alexander Haig, had persuaded Leon Jaworski, a prominent Houston attorney and former president of the American Bar Association, to accept a new special prosecutor position. Jaworski agreed only under the condition that he have complete independence from the White House.

The Impact of the Incident

Jaworski's investigation turned out to be perhaps even more relentless than Cox's. When Nixon continued to resist handing over his tapes, Jaworski took the President to court in a lawsuit that ultimately landed before the Supreme Court of the United States. In a unanimous 1974 decision the court ordered Nixon to comply with Jaworski's subpoena. On August 8, faced with the prospect of public humiliation and criminal indictment, Nixon resigned from office in disgrace.

Many historians agree that the most devastating effect of the Saturday Night Massacre was its undercutting of Nixon's support among all but his most fiercely loyal partisans. Judge John Sirica, who had upheld Cox's demand that the President comply with his subpoena, commented that when FBI agents barred Cox's staff from entering their offices, "it began to look as if some colonels in a Latin American country had staged a coup." This was indeed the prevailing sentiment among Americans, that the administration's actions were simply un-American. By November only 27 percent of Americans rated Nixon's job performance positively. Republican Senators Barry Goldwater of Arizona and James Buckley of New York were so appalled that they openly expressed their own discontent, opening a floodgate of criticism from Republicans in Congress. The White House had crossed a dangerous line, and even the President's own party was in revolt.

Archibald Cox, a Harvard Law School professor who served as President [John F.] Kennedy's solicitor general, found it terrifying that the President of the United States had dismissed the man assigned to investigate him, simply because he was coming too close to the heart of a secret. Reflecting on the events of October 1973 Cox later wrote, "The most important thing was that the rule of law should prevail; the president must comply with the law. Ultimately, all [civil] liberties were at stake." And the American people clearly agreed. Taking to the phones and the wires, the post and the streets, they set aside partisan politics and successfully rose up to defend the supremacy of the law. Within months the President was out of office, and a long process of national healing began.

The Importance of the Presidential Tapes

Mike Feinsilber

Facing enormous political and legal pressure, President Richard M. Nixon was finally forced to release many of the Watergate-related tapes in late July and early August 1974. As Associated Press reporter Mike Feinsilber explains in the following article published by the Houston Chronicle *on June 6, 1997, these presidential tapes, more than anything else, brought down the Nixon presidency. One of the tapes was particularly damaging. This was a conversation Nixon had with White House aide H.R. Haldeman on June 23, 1972, just days after the Watergate burglary, in which Nixon ordered Haldeman to direct the Federal Bureau of Investigation (FBI) to abandon its investigation. This tape soon became known as the "smoking gun" because it confirmed not only that Nixon knew of the cover-up of the Watergate scandal early on, but also that he had directed it. Because of this incontrovertible evidence, Nixon lost the support of many Republicans in Congress, making impeachment likely if he did not resign from the presidency.*

It was a Friday afternoon in July [July 13, 1973], and the witness was just a small fry: Alexander Butterfield, who kept President Nixon's schedule and handled his paper flow. Three staff members of the Senate Watergate Committee were questioning him, preparing for his public testimony the following Monday. Trolling, one asked whether there might be something down at the White House, some sort of recording system? Butterfield took a breath. "I was hoping you fellows wouldn't ask me that," he said. And with that, history turned a corner. What Butterfield revealed that afternoon in 1973—and

Mike Feinsilber, "The Tapes That Ensnared—and Felled—a President," *Houston Chronicle*, June 1997, reprinted with permission of the Associated Press.

on television to the senators and the world three days later—was electrifying news: For 2 and [frac12] years, Nixon had been secretly taping his conversations.

Incontestable Evidence

Five microphones in his desk and two in wall lamps by the fireplace, still more in the Cabinet Room, at his hideaway in the Old Executive Office Building, and at the presidential retreat at Camp David, Md., picked up everything said in Nixon's presence. Now Watergate was no longer the word of one man, White House counsel John Dean [who had testified to Nixon's involvement], against another, Richard Nixon. Now there was incontestable contemporaneous evidence to be had.

Without the tapes, it was unlikely Nixon would have had to give up the presidency. More than anything else that happened in the Watergate scandal—the 25-month drama that brought down a president—Butterfield's disclosure was fatal to Nixon. From that moment, the investigation into those behind the break-in at Democratic Party headquarters in the Watergate building became a battle over access to the tapes.

Nixon's Refusal to Release the Tapes

Nixon fought hard. He fired a special prosecutor, Archibald Cox, who insisted on getting the tapes. He went on television with a pile of looseleaf notebooks that he said contained transcripts of the tapes. "The president has nothing to hide," he said. This "will tell it all." It didn't. He had doctored the transcripts and cleaned up his language. "Expletive deleted" became part of the political and popular lexicon. The ploy failed. The House Judiciary Committee, considering the possibility of impeaching Nixon, joined the special prosecutor in demanding the tapes themselves. Even Nixon's expurgated version damaged him: They showed the president as a vengeful schemer—rambling, undisciplined, mean-spirited and bigoted.

When the Supreme Court, a year after Butterfield spilled the beans, ordered Nixon to surrender the tapes to Cox's successor, Nixon had reached the end of his rope. Refusal surely would have guaranteed his removal from office. And, as it turned out, so would compliance.

The "Smoking Gun"

Two weeks later, Nixon gave up a final tape, made six days after the break-in. It recorded a discussion between Nixon and White House chief of staff H.R. Haldeman. Told that the FBI's investigation was leading to Nixon's re-election campaign, Nixon instructed Haldeman to tell the FBI, "Don't go any further into this case, period."

That was it: evidence that almost from Day One Nixon played a role in the conspiracy to conceal White House involvement. The House Judiciary Committee had already approved three articles of impeachment. But the vote was partisan: Democrats firmly against Nixon, Republicans mostly in support. He could still hope for acquittal in the Senate.

With the release of the incriminating tape—the famous "smoking gun"—Nixon's Republican support in Congress vanished. On Aug. 9, [1974], four days later, Nixon became the first president in history to resign.

The Question of Destruction

Why didn't Nixon destroy the tapes when their existence was revealed—and before they became subpoenaed evidence whose destruction would have been a crime? Nixon would say later that failing to destroy them was his biggest mistake. But he had convinced himself that he would never have to give them up. Moreover, he thought he could use them selectively to bolster his claim that he had nothing to do with Watergate. And he wanted them to write his own version of history.

When Nixon resigned, he sought to take the tapes and his White House papers with him. Newly installed President [Gerald] Ford had the truck stopped from leaving the White House grounds, and Congress passed a law seizing the materials on behalf of the American people. It ordered that those parts that don't concern state secrets or purely personal matters be made public.

Nixon, for the rest of his life, and his estate ever since have fought to keep the tapes from being heard.

Deep Throat Revealed

John D. O'Connor

During their coverage of the Watergate affair, Washington Post reporters Bob Woodward and Carl Bernstein *regularly relied on a secret informant within the government, whom they called Deep Throat. After Nixon's resignation, there was much speculation about the identity of Deep Throat, but Woodward and Bernstein refused to reveal the informant's name. The two reporters kept their secret for decades, and they embellished the mystery in a 1974 best-selling book about their Watergate days called* All the President's Men. *Two years later the book was made into a blockbuster movie starring Robert Redford and Dustin Hoffman as the reporters. Finally, in a July 2005* Vanity Fair *article written by San Francisco lawyer John D. O'Connor, Deep Throat was publicly identified as Mark Felt, former associate director of the FBI.*

The identity of Deep Throat is modern journalism's greatest unsolved mystery. It has been said that he may be the most famous anonymous person in U.S. history. But, regardless of his notoriety, American society today owes a considerable debt to the government official who decided, at great personal risk, to help Woodward and Bernstein as they pursued the hidden truths of Watergate.

The Watergate Break-In

First, some background. In the early-morning hours of June 17, 1972, five "burglars" were caught breaking into the headquarters of the Democratic National Committee at the Watergate complex, along the Potomac River. Two members of the team were found to have address books with scribbles "W

House" and "W.H." They were operating, as it turned out, on the orders of E. Howard Hunt, a onetime C.I.A. agent who had recently worked in the White House, and G. Gordon Liddy, an ex-F.B.I. agent who was on the payroll of the Committee to Re-elect the President (CRP, pronounced Creep, which was organizing Nixon's run against Senator George McGovern, the South Dakota Democrat).

Funds for the break-in, laundered through a Mexican bank account, had actually come from the coffers of CRP, headed by John Mitchell, who had been attorney general during Nixon's first term. Following the break-in, suspicions were raised throughout Washington: What were five men with Republican connections doing with gloves, cameras, large amounts of cash, and bugging equipment in the Democrats' top campaign office?

The case remained in the headlines thanks to the dogged reporting of an unlikely team of journalists, both in their late 20s: Carl Bernstein, a scruffy college dropout and six-year veteran of the *Post* (now a writer, lecturer, and *Vanity Fair* contributor), and Bob Woodward, an ex-navy officer and Yale man (now a celebrated author and *Post* assistant managing editor). The heat was also kept on because of a continuing F.B.I. investigation, headed by the bureau's acting associate director, Mark Felt, whose teams interviewed 86 administration and CRP staffers. These sessions, however, were quickly undermined. The White House and CRP had ordered that their lawyers be present at every meeting. Felt believed that the C.I.A. deliberately gave the F.B.I. false leads. And most of the bureau's "write-ups" of the interviews were being secretly passed on to Nixon counsel John Dean—by none other than Felt's new boss, L. Patrick Gray. (Gray, the acting F.B.I. director, had taken over after J. Edgar Hoover's death, six weeks before the break-in.) Throughout this period, the Nixon camp denied any White House or CRP involvement in the Watergate affair. And after a three-month "investigation" there was no evidence to implicate any White House staffers.

The Watergate probe appeared to be at an impasse, the break-in having been explained away as a private extortion scheme that didn't extend beyond the suspects in custody. McGovern couldn't gain campaign traction with the issue, and the president was re-elected in November 1972 by an overwhelming majority.

The Role of Deep Throat

But during that fateful summer and fall, at least one government official was determined not to let Watergate fade away. That man was Woodward's well-placed source. In an effort to keep the Watergate affair in the news, Deep Throat had been consistently confirming or denying confidential information for the reporter, which he and Bernstein would weave into their frequent stories, often on the *Post*'s front page.

Ever cautious, Woodward and Deep Throat devised cloak-and-dagger methods to avoid tails and eavesdroppers during their numerous rendezvous. If Woodward needed to initiate a meeting, he would position an empty flowerpot (which contained a red construction flag) to the rear of his apartment balcony. If Deep Throat was the instigator, the hands of a clock would mysteriously appear on page 20 of Woodward's copy of *The New York Times*, which was delivered before seven each morning. Then they would connect at the appointed hour in an underground parking garage. The garage afforded Deep Throat a darkened venue for hushed conversation, a clear view of any potential intruders, and a quick escape route.

Whoever Deep Throat might have been, he was certainly a public official in private turmoil. As the two *Post* reporters would explain in their 1974 behind-the-scenes book about Watergate, *All the President's Men*, Deep Throat lived in solitary dread, under the constant threat of being summarily fired or even indicted, with no colleagues in whom he could confide. He was justifiably suspicious that phones had been wire-tapped, rooms bugged, and papers rifled. He was completely isolated, having placed his career and his institution in jeopardy. Eventually, Deep Throat would even warn Woodward and Bernstein that he had reason to believe "everyone's life is in danger"—meaning Woodward's, Bernstein's, and, presumably, his own.

In the months that followed, the *Post* 's exposés continued unabated in the face of mounting White House pressure and protest. Deep Throat, having become more enraged with the administration, grew more bold. Instead of merely corroborating facts that the two reporters obtained from other sources, he began providing leads and outlining an administration-sanctioned conspiracy. (In the film version of the book, Robert Redford and Dustin Hoffman would portray Woodward and Bernstein, while Hal Holbrook assumed the Deep Throat role.)

Soon public outcry grew. Other media outlets began to investigate in earnest. The Senate convened riveting televised hearings in 1973, and when key players such as John Dean cut immunity deals, the entire plot unraveled. President Nixon, it turned out, had tape-recorded many of the meetings where strategies had been hashed out—and the cover-up discussed (in violation of obstruction-of-justice laws). On August 8, 1974, with the House of Representatives clearly moving toward impeachment, the president announced his resignation, and more than 30 government and campaign officials in and around the Nixon White House would ultimately plead guilty to or be convicted of crimes. In brief, Watergate had reaffirmed that no person, not even the president of the United States, is above the law.

Due in no small part to the secrets revealed by the *Post*, sometimes in consort with Deep Throat, the courts and the Congress have been loath to grant a sitting president free rein, and are generally wary of administrations that might try to impede access to White House documents in the name of "executive privilege." Watergate helped set in motion what would become known as the "independent counsel" law (for investigating top federal officials) and helped make whistle-blowing (on wrongdoings in business and government) a legally sanctioned, if still risky and courageous, act. Watergate invigorated an independent press, virtually spawning a generation of investigative journalists.

And yet, ever since the political maelstrom of Nixon's second term, Deep Throat has declined to reveal himself. He has kept quiet through seven presidencies and despite an anticipated fortune that might have come his way from a tell-all book, film, or television special. Woodward has said that Deep Throat wished to remain anonymous until death, and he pledged to keep his source's confidence, as he has for more than a generation. . . .

White House Barriers

As the F.B.I. pushed on with its Watergate investigation, the White House threw up more and more barriers. When Felt and his team believed they could "trace the source of the money that had been in the possession of the Watergate 'burglars'" to a bank in Mexico City, Gray, according to Felt, "flatly ordered [Felt] to call off any interviews" in Mexico because they "might upset" a C.I.A. operation there. Felt and his key deputies sought a meeting with Gray. "Look," Felt recalled telling his boss, "the reputation of the FBI is at stake. . . . Unless we get a request in writing [from the C.I.A.] to forgo the [Mexico] interview, we're going ahead anyway!

"That's not all," Felt supposedly added. "We must do something about the complete lack of cooperation from John Dean and the Committee to Reelect the President. It's obvious they're holding back—delaying and leading us astray in every way they know. We expect this sort of thing when we are in-

Former FBI agent Mark Felt (center), seen here with his daughter Joan Felt and grandson Nick Jones, came forward to reveal he was Watergate informant "Deep Throat." in May 2005. © Lou DeMatteis/Reuters/Corbis

vestigating organized crime. . . . The whole thing is going to explode right in the President's face."

At a subsequent meeting, according to Felt, Gray asked whether the investigation could be confined to "these seven subjects," referring to the five burglars, plus Hunt and Liddy. Felt responded, "We will be going much higher than these seven. These men are the pawns. We want the ones who moved the pawns." Agreeing with this team, Gray chose to stay the course and continue the probe.

Felt's book [a memoir entitled *The F.B.I. Pyramid*] gives no indication that during this same period he decided to go outside the bounds of government to expose the corruption within Nixon's team—or to overcome the impediments they were placing on his ability to do his job. There are only scant clues that he might have decided to pass along secrets to *The Washington Post*; in fact, Felt makes a point of categorically denying he is Deep Throat. But, in truth, the White House had begun asking for Felt's head, even though Gray adamantly defended his deputy. . . .

It is clear from the Watergate tapes that Felt was indeed one of the targets of Nixon's wrath. In October 1972, Nixon insisted he would "fire the whole Goddamn Bureau," and singled out Felt, whom he thought to be part of a plot to undermine him through frequent press leaks. . . .

It was Gray, however, not Felt, who became the fall guy. At Gray's confirmation hearings, in February 1973, he was abandoned by his onetime allies in the West Wing and was left to "twist slowly, slowly in the wind," in the words of Nixon aide John Ehrlichman. With Gray now gone, Felt had lost his last sponsor and protector. Next up was interim F.B.I. director [William] Ruckelshaus, who ultimately resigned as assistant attorney general in Nixon's Saturday Night Massacre. Felt left the bureau that same year and went on the lecture circuit. . . .

Nowadays, Mark Felt watches TV sitting beneath a large oil painting of his late wife, Audrey, and goes for car rides with a new caregiver. Felt is 91 and his memory for details seems to wax and wane. [His daughter] Joan allows him two glasses of wine each evening, and on occasion the two harmonize in a rendition of "The Star-Spangled Banner." While Felt is a humorous and mellow man, his spine stiffens and his jaw tightens when he talks about the integrity of his dear F.B.I.

I believe that Mark Felt is one of America's greatest secret heroes. Deep in his psyche, it is clear to me, he still has qualms about his actions, but he also knows that historic events compelled him to behave as he did: standing up to an executive branch intent on obstructing his agency's pursuit of the truth. Felt, having long harbored the ambivalent emotions of pride and self-reproach, has lived for more than 30 years in a prison of his own making, a prison built upon his strong moral principles and his unwavering loyalty to country and cause. But now, buoyed by his family's revelations and support, he need feel imprisoned no more.

CHAPTER 3

The Legacy
of Watergate

Watergate Was Caused by a Lust for Political Power

Sam J. Ervin Jr.

The Senate Select Committee on Presidential Campaign Activities, commonly called the Senate Watergate Committee, was established on February 7, 1973, to investigate alleged illegal and improper activities that occurred during the 1972 presidential campaign and election. The chairman of the committee was Samuel J. Ervin Jr., a folksy but well-respected senator from North Carolina. During the summer of 1973 the committee held numerous, sometimes spellbinding televised hearings featuring the testimony of various low- and high-ranking employees of the Committee to Re-elect the President (Richard M. Nixon) and of the Nixon White House. In June 1974, shortly before the House Judiciary Committee moved to impeach Nixon, the Ervin Committee released its report to the public. Accompanying the report was a statement from Ervin that summarizes the illegalities in the Watergate affair and states that Watergate was caused by a "lust for political power." Ervin concludes that the antidote to these types of scandals must be moral integrity among the people entrusted with political power.

Watergate was not invented by enemies of the Nixon administration or even by the news media. On the contrary, Watergate was perpetrated upon America by White House and political aides, whom President Nixon himself had entrusted with the management of his campaign for reelection to the Presidency, a campaign which was divorced to a marked degree from the campaigns of other Republicans who sought election to public office in 1972. I note at this point without elaboration that these White House and political aides were

Sam J. Ervin Jr., final report from the U.S. Senate Select Committee on Presidential Campaign Activities, *Final Report*, 93rd Cong., 2d sess., 1974, pp. 1097–1103.

virtually without experience in either Government or politics apart from their association with President Nixon.

Watergate was without precedent in the political annals of America in respect to the scope and intensity of its unethical and illegal actions. To be sure, there had been previous milder political scandals in American history. That fact does not excuse Watergate. Murder and stealing have occurred in every generation since Earth began, but that fact has not made murder meritorious or larceny legal.

What Was Watergate?

Watergate was a conglomerate of various illegal and unethical activities in which various officers and employees of the Nixon reelection committee and various White House aides of President Nixon participated in varying ways and degrees to accomplish these successive objectives:

1. To destroy, insofar as the Presidential election of 1972 was concerned, the integrity of the process by which the President of the United States is nominated and elected.

2. To hide from law enforcement officers, prosecutors, grand jurors, courts, the news media, and the American people the identities and wrongdoing of those officers and employees of the Nixon reelection committees, and those White House aides who had undertaken to destroy the integrity of the process by which the President of the United States is nominated and elected.

To accomplish the first of these objectives. . . .

1. They exacted enormous contributions—usually in cash—from corporate executives by impliedly implanting in their minds the impressions that the making of the contributions was necessary to insure that the corporations would receive governmental favors, or avoid governmental disfavors, while President Nixon remained in the White House. A substantial portion of the contributions were made out of corporate funds in violation of a law enacted by Congress a generation ago.

2. They hid substantial parts of these contributions in cash in safes and safe deposits to conceal their sources and the identities of those who had made them.

3. They disbursed substantial portions of these hidden contributions in a surreptitious manner to finance the bugging and the burglary of the offices of the Democratic National Committee in the Watergate complex in Washington. . . .

4. They deemed the departments and agencies of the Federal Government to be the political playthings of the Nixon administration rather than impartial instruments for serving the people, and undertook to induce them to channel Federal contracts, grants, and loans to areas, groups, or individuals so as to promote the reelection of the President rather than to further the welfare of the people.

5. They branded as enemies of the President individuals and members of the news media who dissented from the President's policies and opposed his reelection, and conspired to urge the Department of Justice, the Federal Bureau of Investigation, the Internal Revenue Service, and the Federal Communications Commission to pervert the use of their legal powers to harass them for so doing.

6. They borrowed from the Central Intelligence Agency disguises which E. Howard Hunt used in political espionage operations, and photographic equipment which White House employees known as the "Plumbers" and their hired confederates used in connection with burglarizing the office of a psychiatrist which they believed contained information concerning Daniel Ellsberg which the White House was anxious to secure.

7. They assigned to E. Howard Hunt, who was at the time a White House consultant occupying an office in the

Executive Office Building, the gruesome task of falsifying State Department documents which they contemplated using in their altered state to discredit the Democratic Party by defaming the memory of former President John Fitzgerald Kennedy, who as the hapless victim of an assassin's bullet had been sleeping in the tongueless silence of the dreamless dust for 9 years.

8. They used campaign funds to hire saboteurs to forge and disseminate false and scurrilous libels of honorable men running for the Democratic Presidential nomination in Democratic Party primaries.

The Cover-Up

During the darkness of the early morning of June 17, 1972, James W. McCord, the security chief of the John Mitchell committee [the Committee to Reelect the President], and four residents of Miami, Fla., were arrested by Washington police while they were burglarizing the offices of the Democratic National Committee in the Watergate complex to obtain political intelligence. . . . The arrest of McCord and the four residents of Miami created consternation in the Nixon reelection committees and the White House. . . . Various White House aides undertook to conceal from law enforcement officers, prosecutors, grand jurors, courts, the news media, and the American people the identities and activities of those officers and employees of the Nixon reelection committee and those White House aides who had participated in any way in the Watergate affair. . . .

1. They destroyed the records of the Nixon reelection committee antedating the bugging and the burglary.

2. They induced the Acting Director of the FBI, who was a Nixon appointee, to destroy the State Department documents which E. Howard Hunt had been falsifying.

3. They obtained from the Acting Director of the FBI copies of the scores of interviews conducted by the FBI

agents in connection with their investigation of the bugging and the burglary, and were enabled thereby to coach their confederates to give false and misleading statements to the FBI.

4. They sought to persuade the FBI to refrain from investigating the sources of the campaign funds which were used to finance the bugging and the burglary.

5. They intimidated employees of the Nixon reelection committees and employees of the White House by having their lawyers present when these employees were being questioned by agents of the FBI, and thus deterred these employees from making full disclosures to the FBI.

6. They lied to agents of the FBI, prosecutors, and grand jurors who undertook to investigate the bugging and the burglary, and to Judge [John] Sirica and the petit jurors who tried the seven original Watergate defendants in January, 1973.

7. They persuaded the Department of Justice and the prosecutors to take out-of-court statements from Maurice Stans, President Nixon's chief campaign fundraiser, and Charles Colson, Egil Krogh, and David Young, White House aides, and Charles Colson's secretary, instead of requiring them to testify before the grand jury investigating the bugging and the burglary in conformity with established procedures governing such matters, and thus denied the grand jurors the opportunity to question them.

8. They persuaded the Department of Justice and the prosecutors to refrain from asking Donald Segretti, their chief hired saboteur, any questions involving Herbert W. Kalmbach, the President's personal attorney, who was known by them to have paid Segretti for dirty tricks he perpetrated upon honorable men seeking the Democratic Presidential nomination. . . .

9. They made cash payments totaling hundreds of thousands of dollars out of campaign funds in surreptitious ways to the seven original Watergate defendants as hush money to buy their silence.

10. They gave assurances to some of the original seven defendants that they would receive Presidential clemency after serving short portions of their sentences if they refrained from divulging the identities and activities of the officers and employees of the Nixon reelection committees and the White House aides who had participated in the Watergate affair.

11. They made arrangements by which the attorneys who represented the seven original Watergate defendants received their fees in cash from moneys which had been collected to finance President Nixon's reelection campaign.

12. They induced the Department of Justice and the prosecutors of the seven original Watergate defendants to assure the news media and the general public that there was no evidence that any persons other than the seven original Watergate defendants were implicated in any way in the Watergate-related crimes.

13. They inspired massive efforts on the part of segments of the news media friendly to the administration to persuade the American people that most of the members of the Select Committee named by the Senate to investigate Watergate were biased and irresponsible men motivated solely by desires to exploit the matters they investigated for personal or partisan advantage. . . .

One shudders to think that the Watergate conspiracies might have been effectively concealed and their most dramatic episode might have been dismissed as a "third-rate" burglary conceived and committed solely by the seven original Watergate defendants had it not been for the courage and penetrating understanding of Judge Sirica, the thoroughness of the investigative reporting of Carl Bernstein, Bob Woodward, and the other representatives of the free press, the labors of the Senate Select Committee and its excellent staff, and the dedication and diligence of Special Prosecutors Archibald Cox and Leon Jaworski and their associates.

Why Was Watergate?

Unlike the men who were responsible for Teapot Dome [a 1920s oil scandal tied to the presidential administration of Warren G. Harding], the Presidential aides who perpetrated Watergate were not seduced by the love of money, which is sometimes thought to be the root of all evil. On the contrary, they were instigated by a lust for political power, which is at least as corrupting as political power itself. . . .

They knew that the power they enjoyed would be lost and the policies to which they adhered would be frustrated if the President should be defeated.

As a consequence of these things, they believed the President's reelection to be a most worthy objective, and succumbed to an age-old temptation. They resorted to evil means to promote what they conceived to be a good end.

Their lust for political power blinded them to ethical considerations and legal requirements; to Aristotle's aphorism that the good of man must be the end of politics; and to [President] Grover Cleveland's conviction that a public office is a public trust.

They had forgotten, if they ever knew, that the Constitution is designed to be a law for rulers and people alike at all times and under all circumstances; and that no doctrine involving more pernicious consequences to the commonweal has ever been invented by the wit of man than the notion that any of its provisions can be suspended by the President for any reason whatsoever.

On the contrary, they apparently believed that the President is above the Constitution, and has the autocratic power to suspend its provisions if he decides in his own unreviewable judgment that his action in so doing promotes his own political interests or the welfare of the Nation. . . .

Antidote for Future Watergates

Is there an antidote which will prevent future Watergates? If so, what is it? . . .

Candor compels the confession . . . that law alone will not suffice to prevent future Watergates. . . .

Law is not self-executing. Unfortunately, at times its execution rests in the hands of those who are faithless to it. And even when its enforcement is committed to those who revere it, law merely deters some human beings from offending, and punishes other human beings for offending. It does not make men good. This task can be performed only by ethics or religion or morality. . . .

When all is said, the only sure antidote for future Watergates is understanding of fundamental principles and intellectual and moral integrity in the men and women who achieve or are entrusted with governmental political power.

The U.S. Constitutional System Worked During Watergate

Mel Elfin

In the following reflection published on the twentieth anniversary of the beginning of the Watergate scandal, Mel Elfin, the editor of U.S. News & World Report, *writes that Watergate was partly responsible for the public's increasing distrust of politicians. He explains, however, that Watergate also produced positive results. The scandal encouraged Congress to reassert the power of the legislative branch, demonstrated the value of the government's separation of powers, and by transferring political power in a peaceful manner during a presidential crisis, showed that the U.S. Constitution works.*

It began . . . as theater of the absurd, a comic opera burglary that might have been staged by [the Three Stooges] Larry, Curly and Moe. It ended—26 months later—in Shakespearean tragedy, the disgrace of a president brought low by the corruptions of power. This was Watergate, a "cancer on the presidency" that metastasized into constitutional crisis, a political melodrama that astonished, amused, angered and shocked a nation still rent by the convulsions of the 1960s. And by the final curtain, it had further eroded confidence in an office already impaired by the amorous escapades of one recent president and the credibility gap of another.

An Abuse of Presidential Power

Watergate was at once Washington morality play and made-for-television mystery that focused not on whodunit but "What did the president know and when did he know it?" Un-

Mel Elfin, "A Scandal's Healing Power," *U.S. News & World Report*, vol. 112, June 22, 1992, p. 42. Copyright 1992 U.S. News and World Report, L.P. All rights reserved. Reprinted with permission.

happily, Richard Nixon knew a great deal more and knew it earlier than he was willing to admit—then or even now, when time has transformed him from unindicted co-conspirator into redoubtable elder statesman.

While a new generation of Americans would be hard put to specify the high crimes and misdemeanors that brought Nixon to the brink of impeachment, the prodigious legacies of the scandal remain, in his familiar phrase, "perfectly clear." Indeed, the current dyspepsia [disgruntlement] of the body politic can be traced, at least in part, to Watergate's plots, lies and audio tapes.

Though scandal is a staple of U.S. statecraft, for breadth of wrongdoing nothing quite matches Watergate. It compelled Nixon to become America's first resigned president, made lawbreakers of more than 30 of his closest aides and friends and bequeathed to the lexicon of politics an all-purpose suffix to denote scandal: "Rubbergate" and "Iraqgate."

Constitutional Balance of Power Restored

But Watergate did more than establish new lows in the abuse of presidential power. The effrontery with which the president's men disregarded the law so outraged public opinion that it spurred the restoration of constitutional balance among the three branches of government by encouraging Congress to reassert its authority after being overpowered by a succession of aggressively muscular presidencies.

As Watergate reinforced the power of the legislative branch, it diminished that of the executive: It became a road marker warning occupants of the Oval Office to respect the limits of presidential authority. Watergate also enhanced the prestige of the judicial branch by reaffirming the principle of judicial review. While some of Nixon's men hinted the White House would defy a Supreme Court order to surrender Oval Office tapes, the threat turned out to be empty posturing.

The scandal also reshaped the political landscape. In 1974, the Democrats captured 291 seats in the House of Representatives, giving it a leftward tilt that only now is dissipating. And while Watergate mythologized the role of investigative reporting, ironically, in the long run it may have damaged the media's image. Not only did it embolden some journalists to assume a stridently adversarial posture toward government, it made others too eager to see minor malfeasances as "the new Watergate" and fostered what many believe has become an over-concentration by the media on the character and private lives of candidates.

The Constitutional System Worked

Perhaps most important, especially for those who blame Washington's current malaise on "divided government," Watergate underscored the importance of the constitutional separation of powers. It was these checks and balances that thwarted those whose disregard of the law was leading the nation down a constitutionally dangerous path. Political power in many hands can be frustratingly inefficient; it is also a bulwark of American democracy.

One of the most crucial tests of a democracy is how it transfers political power. By this standard, the resignation of Richard Nixon as president, 10 months after the resignation of Spiro Agnew as vice president, was America's most crucial political challenge since the Civil War. And on that humid afternoon when Gerald Ford, America's first appointed vice president, succeeded to the presidency, our democracy passed the test. The leadership of the world's most powerful nation shifted from a man who had been elected with 46 million votes to one who had gotten none. Yet the instant Ford promised to "preserve, protect and defend the Constitution," he was "Mr. President." No Nixon loyalists plotted the return of the ancien regime; foreign ministries did not dither over whether to recognize the new government. And it was clear whom the Marine Band had in mind when it struck up "Hail to the Chief."

Perhaps it was Ford himself, the plain-spoken Everyman, who best captured the essence of the simple ritual that had made him America's first accidental president. "Our long national nigthmare is over," Ford reassured his countrymen. "Our Constitution works." Two decades later, it still does. And that, as the nation confronts an election [Bill Clinton vs. George H.W. Bush] that could end in unprecedented constitutional confusion, may prove the most comforting of Watergate's many legacies.

Watergate Caused a Loss of Public Trust in Government

Allen N. Sultan

In a reflection on Watergate written in 1994, two decades after the resignation of Richard Nixon, University of Dayton School of Law professor Allen N. Sultan reviews the history of the Watergate affair and discusses both the positive and negative legacies of Watergate. Sultan affirms that the U.S. constitutional system worked. He argues, however, that Watergate may have eroded people's faith in the rule of law. In Sultan's view, when government becomes the lawbreaker it breeds contempt for law among the public, which can undermine the foundations of government itself. Sultan concludes that Watergate provided a clear example of the dangers of indifference and the need for vigilance in the defense of American freedoms.

Two decades have passed since the resignation of Richard Nixon in the aftermath of the break-in at Democratic Party offices at the Watergate complex polarized the American people. Passions, however, usually are transient. The soothing effects of time offer inspection free of the divisive partisan politics that frequently accompany such precipitative events. Today, it is possible to reflect more coolly upon the trying months of Watergate, not as a political crisis, but, rather, as a most important event in the history and constitutional philosophy of the nation.

"I believe this [to be] the strongest government on earth. . .; the only one where every man . . . would fly to the standard of the law, and would meet invasions of the public order as his own personal concern," stated Thomas Jefferson in his inaugural address, March 4, 1801.

On Oct. 18, 1973, the American people rose as one and "flew to the standard of the law" with an avalanche of telegrams to Washington, D.C., that would have made Jefferson and his colleagues swell with pride. Responding to what has become known as "The Saturday Night Massacre," they confirmed Jefferson's confidence and prediction that they "would meet an invasion of the public order as [their] own personal concern." They were, in effect, 20th-century minutemen (and women), armed with their freedoms of expression and petition, rather than a musket. On behalf of themselves and posterity, they kept faith with the heritage of liberty secured by the constitutional rule of law. . . .

The Transgressions of Nixon

Yet, how many, especially the voters of tomorrow, remember or have since learned about the transgressions of Richard Nixon and his immediate subordinates? Consider, as illustrations:

- An enemies list, declaring certain citizens to be "enemies" because they may not agree with some of the policies of their public servants.

- The political surveillance of citizens—the violations of their private lives and personal communications because they may hold independent views of public policy.

- Attempts at special tax audits to destroy various citizens whose only crime was to disagree with those who were temporarily in power.

- The stamp of national security and the claim of "implied powers" that were misused time and again for political gain.

- The sale of government favors—a premeditated campaign of Nixon officialdom furrowing out customers.

Like so many magazine salesmen, they sought their patron in his nest with the message: Buy a piece of the people's government—or else! (Not surprisingly, the manager of that effort, former Secretary of Commerce Maurice Stans, proved to be the most successful money-raiser in the history of American politics.)

- A top government position being dangled before a Federal judge who was presiding over a major trial involving the reach or extent of the powers of the presidency.

- A secret, huge cache of funds to be used at the whim of those in power.

- Key documents involving possible criminal fraud that, for some strange reason, simply could not be found.

- An incredible series of "flip-flops" by Nixon, one time claiming to have acted as president, another as an individual—whichever would have best served his particular dilemma at the time.

- Being told that seeking out the truth would permanently wound the office of the presidency, when, in fact, the President held the integrity of that office in his own hands. (All he had to do was speak the truth.)

- Being told about Nixon's two luxurious estates, of his half-million dollars in back taxes, of his White House guards ostentatiously dressed in the manner befitting the Austrian Hapsburgs, of blasting trumpets announcing his entrance at state dinners, and of the exorbitant refitting of Air Force One so his family would not have to pass through a public area on the plane.

- The deepest cut of all, the desecration of the vote—the refutation of democracy itself—by dirty tricks, burglary, and similar acts amounting to a vast conspiracy to destroy the fundamental constitutional right of all citizens to their free choice in an election.

Nixon's Stonewalling

After these many experiences, Americans still clung to their trust in the rule of law and the system it had created. They patiently awaited action by the Special Prosecutor, Archibald Cox, an eminent constitutional authority at Harvard Law School. Upon taking office, Cox immediately sought out the evidence, no matter where it might lead.

The White House responded with unkept promises, delays, and general deception and evasion, building a stone wall between the White House and the people it served. On March 22, 1973, almost seven months before the Saturday Night Massacre, Nixon instructed Attorney General John Mitchell: "I want you to stonewall it, plead the Fifth Amendment, cover up or anything else."

Cox was fully aware of the compelling significance of his responsibilities to the future efficacy of the republic. He persisted, actively seeking out audio tapes of relevant White House conversations. Then, with the President and the Special Prosecutor eyeball to eyeball, Nixon stumbled, firing Cox. With him went Attorney General Elliot Richardson and his deputy, William Ruckelshaus, both resigning rather than carry the odious message.

With these dismissals on Oct. 18, 1973, Richard Nixon had crossed his Rubicon. By precipitating the Saturday Night Massacre, he had sealed his own fate. The voters were appalled. Political reality mandated that a new Special Prosecutor be appointed—and soon! The public outcry was uniform and vociferous.

Nixon Continues the Fight

The newly appointed Special Prosecutor, Leon Jaworski, a Texas attorney, continued the investigation in the manner and spirit of his predecessor. . . . Ever the political combatant, Nixon fought back:

- He offered a collection of transcripts of White House conversations concerning the break-in on national television and told the American people that they contained the complete facts. In truth, they were replete with distortions and omissions, as later proven by House of Representatives' transcripts of key, unedited tapes.

- The transcripts also evidenced no White House concern for the presidency, national security, or the operations of government—causing some historians later to characterize them as "the most self-incriminating document ever published by an American president."

- On a human level, the language of the President and his advisors astonished and outraged the American people. Most significantly, Nixon's words were "foul, vengeful and full of ethnic slurs . . . [reflecting both] fear and hate."

- When pressured to release the actual tapes, he responded with the claim that some were completely missing—in an administration where every moment was the subject of a memo and every presidential murmur an object for posterity.

- Nixon also wanted the public to accept unbelievable physical contortions by his personal secretary, followed by "a denial theory"—all in an attempt to explain erasures on other tapes that just happened to encompass extremely vital conversations.

- On July 24, 1974, a unanimous Supreme Court ruled that Nixon must release all of the actual audio tapes.

- Also on July 24, at 7:45 p.m., Rep. Peter Rodino (D.-N.J.), chairman of the House Judiciary Committee, rapped his gavel on nationwide television, opening the hearings that commenced the impeachment process. He said, "Make no mistake about it. This is a turning point—whatever we decide. . . . [O]ur judgment is not concerned with an individual but with a system of constitutional government. . . . We have been fair. Now the American people, the House of Representatives, and the whole history of our republic demand that we make up our minds."

- Members of the committee then made their positions known. For instance, Rep. Barbara Jordan (D.-Tex.) declared, "My faith in the Constitution is whole, it is complete, it is total, and I am not going to sit here and be an idle spectator to the diminution, the subversion, the destruction of the Constitution." Rep. James Mann (D.-S.C.) stated, "If there be no accountability, another president will feel free to do as he chooses. The next time there may be no watchman in the night."

- Now completely in a corner, Nixon released more tapes on Aug. 5 [1974]. They revealed that he was directly involved in the cover-up—in the criminal obstruction of justice. One of them has come to be known as the "smoking gun" tape of a White House conversation of June 23, 1972. It contains Nixon's voice clearly directing his aide to demand that the CIA do whatever it can to restrain the FBI's investigation of Watergate. "Call the CIA people and tell them that further inquiry might lead to the whole Bay of Pigs thing." The CIA should call Acting FBI Director Patrick Gray and say, "Don't go further into this case. Period!"

The Scandal Ends

Three days later, finding himself without any political support, Nixon resigned the presidency, effective the next day, Aug. 9, 1974. Thus ended the ominous ordeal known as Watergate.

Although he had been respected for his political sagacity, Nixon's Saturday Night Massacre remains the most prominent example of the dangers of confusing knowledge with wisdom. His ill-fated decisions of that evening triggered a pervasive nationwide reaction that led to his inevitable fall from power. In the last analysis, Nixon lost his furious gamble because he did not understand the values of the nation and the attitudes of the people that he led, and because his acts were a dramatic insight into his true character.

To the amazement of much of the rest of the world, the most powerful office on Earth changed hands peaceably. True to the motto on the national seal—Novus Ordo Seclorum (a new cycle of the ages)—the U.S. still was teaching the rest of the world by example. The institutions of government remained firm; the soldiers remained in their barracks; the system based upon freedom of expression for both citizen and the press protected by an independent judiciary fully worked, as the Framers knew it would; and the constitutional rule of law prevailed.

The cashiering of a sitting president remains a momentous event. A sobering message can be inferred from the fact that no president ever had been forced out of office in almost 200 years until Nixon was. . . .

The Lessons of Watergate

Why, after two decades, look back at Watergate? Since Nixon paid a significant price for his obviously improper behavior, why not simply focus upon the numerous contemporary challenges?

To respond properly requires asking a further question: What have been the empirical effects of Watergate on U.S. society and on Americans' personal day-to-day interactions with each other and their government? If there have been no serious ongoing detriments from the national trauma, Watergate should be relegated to the history books. In that circumstance, there would be no need to (in Nixon's words) "wallow in Watergate."

However, if there has been and continues to be serious permanent damage to our society from Watergate, then we should (indeed, must) periodically review the very important lessons it teaches about the possible base abuse of political power so feared by the Founding Fathers. . . .

Simple common sense suggests the greatest harmful legacy of Watergate—the possible erosion of faith in the rule of law. Probably the best articulation of the underlying relevant principle of political philosophy and its psychological ramifications on individual citizens came from the pen of Supreme Court Justice Louis Brandeis:

> Decency, security and liberty alike demand that government officials shall be subjected to the same rules of conduct that are commands to the citizen. In a government of laws, existence of the government will be imperiled if it fails to observe the law scrupulously. Our government is the potent, the omnipresent teacher. For good or for ill, it teaches the whole people by its example. Crime is contagious. If the government becomes a lawbreaker, it breeds contempt for law; it invites every man to become a law unto himself; it invites anarchy.

Admittedly, abuse of power, greed, and corruption are indigenous to human affairs, infesting leaders as well as many of those they, in theory, serve. Yet, Watergate remains in a class by itself. Its many characteristics cause it to be set apart from other political criminal enterprises. Its felons commanded the very apex of the political hierarchy; their crimes were so blatant; their ongoing conspiracies included so many culpable individuals; their arrogance towards their fellow citizens, including some of their own colleagues, at times challenged human imagination; their criminal activities continued for such a long time; and they executed so many crimes against social order.

These differences in degree have given Watergate its unique status, making it the pithy teacher of the present and future generations. It elucidates the necessity for diligence and demonstrates the dangers of indifference: That we all pay a steep price when we ignore Jefferson's call for "external vigilance" in the cause of freedom. . . . Like polluted soil and water, the national psyche eventually will be purified of the insidious defilement by the Watergate legacy. However, it undoubtedly will take a long, long time.

Watergate Harmed the Journalism Profession

Alicia C. Shepard

In an article published in the American Journalism Review *twenty-five years after Watergate, journalist and writer Alicia C. Shepard examines the effect the scandal has had on the journalism profession. According to Shepard, Watergate made reporters Bob Woodward and Carl Bernstein famous and spawned a new era of celebrity journalism, in which a few journalists have become wealthy and sometimes as well known as the people they cover. This phenomenon of celebrity, Shepard says, causes the public to lose its respect for the profession. Although many celebrity journalists are well-qualified reporters who have paid their dues, she argues, some journalists today are becoming overnight celebrities whose qualifications are sometimes questionable. Shepard concludes that, overall, the changes in journalism that began with Watergate have harmed the profession.*

The Watergate affair changed journalism in many ways, not the least of which was by launching the era of the journalist as celebrity. Woodward and Bernstein, portrayed, respectively, by Robert Redford and Dustin Hoffman in the movie *All the President's Men*, were pioneers in the now widespread phenomenon in which a handful of wealthy, glamorous journalists are as famous, if not more famous, than the people they cover.

Celebrity Journalists

"Celebrity journalists," a phrase coined in 1986 by James Fallows, abound these days, on television and in print. *People* magazine writes about them. *Vanity Fair* offers up flattering

Alicia C. Shepard, "Celebrity Journalists," *American Journalism Review*, vol. 19, September 1997. Reproduced by permission of the author.

profiles. Their names appear in gossip columns and on society pages. When they come to small towns simply doing their jobs, their arrival can become front page news. We know when they wed (witness the union of Garry Trudeau and Jane Pauley), when they become parents (Connie Chung and Maury Povich's struggles with infertility and eventual adoption captivated *People* magazine readers) and when they get divorced (Peter Jennings and Kati Marton).

"A celebrity journalist is a journalist whose nose has risen above the wall for various reasons," former *Washington Post* Executive Editor (and celebrity journalist) Ben Bradlee said at a Freedom Forum seminar on Watergate and Celebrity Journalism in June [1997]. "Generally the story has taken him or her there. The first thing you can say about it is it exists, and to recognize that it exists is important. The second thing you can say is that, without television, we could write up a storm and sell a million papers a day on it, but that won't get you to be a celebrity journalist except on your own block. The third thing is it's not all bad. It sure as hell isn't all good, but it isn't all bad. It opens a lot of doors."

When Arthur Kent covered the [1991] Persian Gulf War for NBC, he became known as the "Scud Stud." Everyone remembers CNN war correspondent nonpareil Peter Arnett broadcasting live from Iraq with bombs bursting around him. And this summer [1997] more has been printed about CNN anchor Bernard Shaw's appearances in the movies *The Lost World* and *Contact* than about anything he's done as a journalist.

A celebrity, writes Daniel J. Boorstin, historian and former head of the Library of Congress, "is a person who is known for his well-knownness." And, he adds in an interview, "journalists are the creators of well-knownness. In the process of creating well-knownness for others, it's not surprising that some of them become celebrities too. It's inevitable."

A Decline in Public Confidence

Few journalists embrace the celebrity label. Woodward scoffs at the notion that he's one. But that's not how the public sees it. The public reads about journalists dining at the White House, inviting Colin Powell over for dinner, sending their kids to school with Chelsea Clinton, playing tennis with presidential assistants, partying with Hollywood stars at affairs like the White House Correspondents Dinner, receiving mind-boggling fees for hour-long speaking engagements and spouting off on TV and radio on subjects they know little or nothing about. And while the media elite is a tiny slice of the profession, it plays a major role in shaping the public's negative perception of the press.

"The public feels that journalists are too aggressive in the way they play their watchdog role, and they are doing it not because they are seeking the truth but to advance their careers," says Andrew Kohut, director of the Pew Research Center for the People & the Press. "The notion that journalists were of the people, as was the case 30 or 40 years ago, is no longer the case because of the rise of celebrity journalism. I don't think this is the issue that most hurts journalism, but it's one of a cluster of things that has eroded the public confidence in the press."

Adds journalism reformer Fallows, now editor of *U.S. News & World Report*, "I don't think I'd put it [celebrity journalism] on the top five list of major problems for journalism right now. By definition, it only affects an elite. But it is a problem because it aggravates other sources of people being mad at us—and therefore not listening to what we say or do."

Famous for Their Reporting or TV Exposure?

Most media celebrities hail from the world of television. Peter Jennings, Ted Koppel, Sam Donaldson, Cokie Roberts, Diane Sawyer and Barbara Walters of ABC; Katie Couric . . . , Tom

Brokaw, Jane Pauley, Tim Russert and Stone Phillips of NBC; Dan Rather, Ed Bradley and Mike Wallace of CBS; Wolf Blitzer, Bernard Shaw and Judy Woodruff of CNN; Fox's Brit Hume and CNBC's Geraldo Rivera. These are journalists who have paid their dues. They didn't burst out of the box as celebrities. But there's a new generation of journalists who have become overnight stars. Perhaps the best example is MTV's Tabitha Soren. . . .

So what makes someone a celebrity journalist, and how does one obtain that lofty status? "A celebrity journalist is someone who is famous for who they are instead of what they report," says media analyst S. Robert Lichter, director of the Center for Media and Public Affairs. "There's a spectrum going from journalists who are unknown to the pure celebrities whose journalism is irrelevant, like Geraldo Rivera. There are clearly celebrity journalists who are good reporters but whose celebrity is based upon [television exposure]. Dan Rather is both a celebrity and a good journalist."

John Carmody, who has written a TV column for the *Washington Post* for 20 years, says the key is "your willingness to become a celebrity. There's a lot of very solid journalists in television who keep their mouths shut and don't let their personal lives get into anything and don't sit still for interviews. But some of these people won't take the money and shut up. They have to appear on every panel and show up on all the talk shows." . . .

At the Freedom Forum seminar, *Baltimore Sun* columnist Jules Witcover pointed out that celebrity journalists come in two very distinct flavors: those who, like Bob Woodward, earn that status from exemplary work, and those who become famous simply because they appear on television.

Lichter cites the contrasting approaches of Woodward and Bernstein. "Bob Woodward," says Lichter, "is more of the old school, like Nelly Bly and Richard Harding Davis. They were journalists who, by virtue of breaking enormous stories, became public figures."

Bernstein, Lichter notes, became a public figure thanks to his Watergate coverage and then chose a different route. "Look at Carl Bernstein, who became one of the beautiful people. Where are the important works of journalism from Carl Bernstein in recent years? Woodward remained the traditional hard-working journalist, whereas Bernstein became part of the celebrity culture."

Woodward has tried to shun celebrityhood by not going on every talk show that invites him, speaking publicly only on subjects he's written books about or is reporting on. He's not a fan of "food fight" television. "I think it's a waste of time to sit around and talk about something you don't know anything about," he says.

Asked if he considers himself a celebrity, he responds quickly: "I sure don't." Long pause; Woodward clearly is uncomfortable. "I really love reporting. It's one of the great jobs." So he continues working as an editor at the *Post* and writing books.

Bernstein, on the other hand, never shied away from the glitz. "After Nixon's resignation and *All the President's Men*," Michael Kilian wrote in 1991, "Bernstein went on to an unsuccessful career as a TV-Network bureau chief and correspondent, but a lasting one as a professional celebrity." . . .

Despite their differences, the Watergate duo together played a major role in launching the current incarnation of the journalist as star. "Woodward and Bernstein seemed to start the trend where there's a lot more interest in the reporter than there ever seemed to be," says Maurine Beasley, who teaches journalism at the University of Maryland. "The publication of their book *All the President's Men* showed the public is more interested in learning about the people who get the news."

Not a New Trend

But the public has always been fascinated by people who report the news, says Mitchell Stephens, journalism professor at New York University and author of *A History of News.* In the 1930s and '40s, Walter Winchell, father of the newspaper gossip column, not only made people celebrities but was himself an influential and well-known figure. The focus shifted, however, from print journalists to their television counterparts as America became a TV-saturated culture.

"I see no evidence that journalists are better known than they were in the past . . . ," Stephens says. "We look at the journalism stars of our own era—Peter Jennings, Geraldo, Woodward and Bernstein—and we think, 'Oh my God, there's no one who was ever that famous before.' But our historical understanding of journalism is very limited."

Until the television era, print journalists were the celebrities. Figures like Richard Harding Davis, Horace Greeley, Nelly Bly, Ida Tarbell, Dorothy Thompson, William Randolph Hearst, E.W. Scripps and Joseph Pulitzer were some of the giants in the field. "Because of their power, Hearst, Pulitzer and Scripps were major celebrities of their time," . . .

But with television, the celebrity machine began to crank up, albeit slowly: TV reporters often were treated like second-class citizens until the early to mid-1960s, according to Lichter. But then came the dramatic footage of the civil rights movement and later the war in Vietnam, and journalists began to take a more prominent role.

"In the 1970s, there was a creation of a star system in journalism the same way there became a star system in the movies at the beginning of the century," Lichter says. He adds that the era of celebrity journalism may have officially begun in 1976, "when Barbara Walters became the first million-dollar anchor on ABC. A million dollars a year was unheard of. I still personally remember the big flap because she had a hairdresser." . . .

The phenomenon also was fueled by the advent of television newsmagazines, "60 Minutes" in particular. Journalists began appearing in mini-news dramas, not just as reporters on the sidelines, but as the good guys going after the bad guys. As the old line goes, there were few sentences in the English language more terrifying than the words, "Mike Wallace is at the door." . . .

Enhancing or Hurting the Profession?

So is the advent of the celebrity journalist a serious problem for the profession? "I'm sure celebrity journalism contributes to the public mistrust," says Robert Giles, former publisher of the *Detroit News* who is executive director of the Freedom Forum's Media Studies Center in New York City. "I think the public sees some of these people as having large egos not unlike those in show business. So they become seen in the same context as other entertainment figures, as celebrities. And I think that's antithetical to the role of journalism. We all know who the cast of characters are who are making speeches and getting fees, and when there is an event, they are as much a part of the event as the event themselves." When they were in Hong Kong recently, he adds, "Tom Brokaw and Dan Rather were celebrities."

But can they help being celebrities? Brokaw has worked for NBC for 31 years. He may be known for his well-knownness, but he's also known as a competent, reliable journalist. It's what a journalist does with his or her celebrity that enhances or hurts the profession. CBS' Mike Wallace, for example, has chosen to use his well-knownness to try to find ways to make journalism more accountable to its audience, pushing for establishment of a national news council.

"Simply the fact that someone has become well-known isn't unto itself either wrong or bad," says [director of Northwestern University's News Management Center John] Lavine. "What we want to make judgments about is what kind of journalists are they? How credible are they? How much energy do they put into maintaining their credibility and caring about the public's confidence?"

If you remain true to the craft and don't exploit your well-knownness, Woodward says, celebrity is unimportant. "I'm not saying celebrity journalism doesn't exist," he says. "I'm saying it shouldn't exist if it inhibits the work, and reporting takes time. And that time is not spent expounding on the theory of the Clinton presidency on television. It's finding out what they really are doing."

Overshadowing the Talented Journalists

Celebrity status can be good for journalism, says Fallows. "The mere fact of books coming out from Tom Wolfe, David Halberstam or Bob Woodward is news because of interest in the author as much as the subject," Fallows says. "People watch or listen to radio or TV shows because they enjoy the approach— even the timbre—of certain well-known correspondents. This is actually good for journalism. The people are well-known based mainly on something in their work, and their renown gets people to pay attention to the news."

But when they use their renown simply to promote themselves, celebrity journalists can't be good for journalism. *Time* magazine asked high school students in South Lake Tahoe, California, whom they thought they could trust. The results: parents first, journalists dead last. "Celebrity journalism has certainly contributed to the problem of trust in journalists," says Diane M. Dusick, head of the communications department at San Bernardino Valley College in California. "It's very sad," Dusick adds. "When I was growing up in the 1960s and '70s, journalists were the be all and end all. Their job was to seek truth. Now they look for the big story that will get me attention, and the truth comes second."

The sad truth is that the elite journalists who appear in movies and high-profile magazines don't represent the profession as a whole, yet they command so much attention that it can seem that way. They overshadow people like Judy Woodruff or Bob Woodward or Jules Witcover, who are known but don't trade on their journalistic credentials to enhance themselves; and on the countless other journalists who do their jobs well on the sidelines.

Thirteen years ago Charles Bailey, then editor of Minneapolis' *Star-Tribune*, presciently predicted the trouble this small segment of the media might cause. Bailey urged journalists to do something to "keep the privileged few from giving the rest of the news business a bad name." That hasn't proven to be an easy task.

The Watergate Scandal Failed to Produce Meaningful Campaign Finance Reform

Brooks Jackson

In an article for Cable News Network (CNN) written on June 17, 1997, reporter Brooks Jackson sums up the effect the Watergate scandal had on the financing of political campaigns. As Jackson explains, Watergate exposed an ugly secret of American politics—that both the Democratic and Republican parties were financed by illegal, underground contributions. Following the scandal, reforms were enacted to fix the problem, and beginning with the 1976 presidential election, only public money was to be used to finance campaigns. Since then, however, court decisions and election commission rulings have largely gutted these reforms and allowed the system to, once again, become corrupt. A consequence of Watergate, Jackson believes, is that the public sees government as untrustworthy and ruled by money. This has undermined the democratic process, he opines, leading many people to forgo voting for any candidate.

The Watergate burglars had rubber gloves on their hands and hundred-dollar bills in their pockets—campaign money that led from the Watergate to President Richard Nixon's re-election committee, and then to the sordid secret of American politics: Illegal, underground financing of both parties.

A total of 21 corporations were found guilty of illegal giving to Republicans and Democrats, including American Airlines, Ashland Oil, Braniff Airways, Carnation Company, Goodyear, Gulf, Hertz and Northrop.

Brooks Jackson, "A Watergate Legacy: More Public Skepticism, Ambivalence," *CNN*, June 13, 1997. Reproduced by permission.

Temporary Campaign Finance Reform

The scandal produced reform—for a while. Only clean money in the election of 1976: nothing over $1,000 in presidential primaries; only public money in the general election between Jimmy Carter and Gerald Ford; and a new Federal Election Commission to police the rules. But it didn't last. Says Brookings Institution scholar Thomas Mann, "We were better off for a while, but we've lost that advantage and now we're at a position where the law as interpreted by the courts and by the politicians permits behavior that we found absolutely appalling in the Watergate era."

The Supreme Court has ruled that money is speech protected by the First Amendment. And the election commission issued regulations allowing "soft money" from corporations, labor unions, and big donors. So [twenty-five years later], more special-interest money than Richard Nixon ever dreamed of—$124 million in soft money to Democrats, $138 million to Republicans—flowed into the two major parties. And, this time, it was mostly legal.

"There is a lot of political ingenuity out there, and any rule you have you can find ways to evade it legally—that's what politicians have done," said Stephen Wayne of Georgetown University. Disclosure still works, maybe too well. What seemed a scandal then is old news now. So much money. And neither side will change: each blames the other.

Other Effects of Watergate

Campaign finance reforms were not the only things to go sour. Watergate also produced systematic efforts to root out corruption. But watchdogs became attack dogs. Hearings paid off for Democrats. They gained 49 seats in the House and four in the Senate in 1974, and one in the White House in 1976. Investigations paid off for reporters, too. They became heroes, some rich and famous. Says Wayne, "The press no longer gives public officials the benefit of the doubt. They think it's all talk to protect their own ego and re-election chances, and they assume if a person is not lying, he's not telling the whole truth."

Practically anything triggers massive investigations: A money-losing real-estate deal such as Bill and Hillary Clinton's Whitewater venture; a college course with a political message, such as that of [former] House Speaker Newt Gingrich; nine million dollars spent to investigate former Agriculture Department Secretary Mike Espy, who may have taken free football tickets.

"We now criminalize what in the old days would have been normal political give-and-take," said Brookings' Mann. "We have the independent counsel law, we have the public integrity section of the Justice Department, we have ethics committees and procedures, we have a lot invested now in detecting wrong-doing."

Loss of Public Trust

Watergate exposed lies, crimes, corruption. The investigation established that no president is above the law. Now many say government is more honest, presidents more accountable. But the public believes government is corrupt, untrustworthy and ruled by money and personal ambition. Last November [1996], only 49 percent even bothered to vote. So after 25 years we're still feeling the effects. More money. Less trust. Fewer voters.

Unmasking Deep Throat Was Irrelevant to the Meaning of Watergate

Stanley I. Kutler

In 2005 the identity of Deep Throat, Bob Woodward and Carl Bernstein's secret informant during their reporting on the Watergate scandal, was revealed to be former FBI agent Mark Felt. Even before then, in a June 18, 2002, article published in Slate, *an online political magazine, University of Wisconsin law professor and Watergate analyst Stanley I. Kutler criticizes the public's fascination with Deep Throat and says Deep Throat was largely irrelevant to the meaning of Watergate. During the Watergate affair, Kutler says, government leaks were rampant and came from many different sources. The real lessons of Watergate, according to Kutler, are that government institutions worked, that Congress did its job in an intelligent and bipartisan manner, and that the court system functioned admirably.*

Current opinion polls reveal that two-thirds of Americans do not know enough about Watergate to discuss it. Based on the tenor of the recent 30th-anniversary observance [in 2002], it's not surprising. Once again, we have been subjected to an orgy of media fascination with Deep Throat. Deep Throat has become a convenient means of journalistic self-congratulation, a way the media reminds us of its place at the center of the Watergate constellation. Only the vigilant diligence of our intrepid reporters, we are told, parted the veil on Watergate and revealed the myriad abuses of power and the criminality of the Richard Nixon administration. It seems that false as well as plagiarized history abounds these days.

Stanley I. Kutler, "Watergate Remembered: The Shallow Debate About Deep Throat," *Slate*, June 18, 2002. Reproduced by permission of the author.

Many Leaks During Watergate

The perpetrator of the notion that the identity of Deep Throat matters appears on the Sunday morning talk show ghetto, smiling contentedly while refusing to divulge the identity of the culprit/hero but promising again to reveal the identity when *he* dies. . . . The mystery deepens.

But, what mystery? That someone leaked to Woodstein [the team of Woodward and Bernstein]? How shocking! The Watergate leaks began almost immediately after the break-in. The National Archives houses more than 10,000 pages of raw FBI field reports that appeared in some Washington newspaper offices a few days after the burglary. [FBI director] J. Edgar Hoover had died in May [1972], and the White House dispatched a loyal Nixonian, L. Patrick Gray, to serve as acting director. After June 20 [1972], Gray cooperated with the CIA to thwart the investigation and kept the White House informed of the bureau's activities. Hoover's loyal hierarchy remained in place, profoundly unhappy with events. So, the Hooverites did what all disgruntled bureaucrats do: They leaked. What distinguished the *Washington Post* from other papers was its eagerness to report the news as the investigation unfolded, which sometimes meant revealing unsubstantiated or simply wrong information. Still, the *Post* reported it.

The U.S. attorney's office for the District of Columbia promptly involved itself, led particularly by Assistant U.S. Attorney Earl Silbert. That office had its own interests to pursue, and leaks were an established mechanism for pursuing them. Silbert himself seems to have leaked very little, carefully distancing himself from reporters, thereby earning their enmity and hostility. Another assistant U.S. attorney, however, could easily qualify as Aunt Blabby. By February 1973, Sen. Sam Ervin, six of his fellow senators, and a staff of more than 100 began the work of the Senate Select Committee [SSC]. The SSC's brilliant efforts, eliciting testimony from the president's men, drove the soaps off the air and made Watergate a national phenomenon. John Mitchell, the former attorney general, campaign manager, and Nixon law partner, acknowledged the "White House horrors" of the previous four years and added that he would have done nearly anything to ensure Nixon's re-election. Obsequious Bob Haldeman desperately tried to portray himself as a grand fellow, not just "the President's son-of-a bitch." Who can forget the incredible arrogance of John Ehrlichman, who defiantly told the committee that no one really cared about presidential respect for the Constitution or the notion that a man's house is his castle? (Georgia Sen. Herman Talmadge's drawling response: "Folks in my part of the country do.") Or that incredible virtuoso performance of memory by John W. Dean, formerly the ringmaster of the cover-up, who now decided to step forward and tell the truth? Richard Nixon himself ultimately vindicated the truth of Dean's testimony when we learned he had bugged himself and had to surrender his tapes.

The SSC did outstanding work but—eager to promote and advance its cause, aides, and maybe the senators themselves—regularly leaked. A few years ago, I appeared on a panel with Sam Dash and Fred Thompson, respectively, the committee's majority and minority counsels. Thompson had become a movie actor of some note (this was before he became a senator himself). When queried about Deep Throat by the audience, I responded that the question was inconsequential—there were many leakers. Shocked, the questioner turned to Dash and asked if that was true. "Leak?" Dash said; "I leaked all the time. Everybody did."

From May 1973 until Nixon's resignation in August 1974, Special Prosecutors Archibald Cox and Leon Jaworski pursued Watergate through the legal process. They also regularly timed leaks to serve their purpose. Toward the end, the House Judiciary Committee held its impeachment hearings, and it, too, leaked like a sieve. And let us not forget the White House itself. Leonard Garment, an aide and sometime counsel to the president, regularly met with reporters. His daily calendar is replete with appointments that included the best-known of the Washington press corps. John Osborne of the *New Republic* was a particular favorite—and it is no accident that Osborne's reporting easily outdistanced the work of his counterparts. Garment and others in the White House (most notably Chief of Staff Alexander Haig) regularly leaked, largely to defuse upcoming bad news—"spin control," we now call it. A few years ago, Garment tried to make a big splash with his own convoluted search for Deep Throat. The story had no legs whatsoever.

The Real Importance of Watergate

The real story of Watergate is infinitely richer and more complex than the press-centric version. We essentially know what happened, but we continue to unravel and expand the complexity, motivations, and meaning of Watergate. New materials emerge, and our insights grow. The new tapes, for example, amplify Nixon's determination to maintain the cover-up. John Dean famously talked with the president on March 21, 1973, warning him of a "cancer on the presidency" and urging him to come forth with the truth. But we now know that as soon as Dean left the Oval Office, Nixon called in his secretary and asked her for "substantial cash for a personal purpose"—that is, his need to pay "hush money" to the burglars. A real Watergate mystery—one worthy of our attention—centers on Nixon's stubborn refusal to "come clean," acknowledge his involvement in the Watergate crimes, and perhaps then, in typical Nixonian fashion, remind Americans that he—not [his election opponent] George McGovern—had saved Americans from Communists, rapists, pot, and sundry other evils.

We now know from the new tapes that the president simply could not confront the truth about the "Plumbers" [aides ordered to stop the leaks] and his authorization of a break-in: "I ordered that they use any means necessary, including illegal means", and then he hastily added: "The President of the United States can *never* admit this." His quarter-century pose as the champion of "law and order" simply trumped his moral center. Would that the media had devoted as much energy to opening Nixon's papers and tapes as it has to prattling about the potential identity of Deep Throat.

Important lessons about Watergate remain to be learned. The institutions of government, established ones as well as some resurrected for the moment, such as the special prosecutor, did their work and did it well. Congress behaved intelligently, soberly, and in bipartisan fashion, setting a pattern that sadly has not been followed in recent decades. The first 37 days of hearings by the Senate Select Committee stand as an exemplary congressional investigation. Special Prosecutor Leon Jaworski, who led Texas Democrats for Nixon in 1972, should be remembered for his heroic achievement. The United States Supreme Court, in a unanimous opinion (Justice [William] Rehnquist recusing himself), delivered its most historic opinion on executive privilege when it ruled that Nixon had to surrender the subpoenaed tapes.

Those are the stories to remember. How they happened and why they happened are live historical questions, of far greater significance than the endless, pointless game of trying to identify Deep Throat.

Appendix of Important Figures in the Watergate Affair

Carl Bernstein Bernstein was a journalist and investigative reporter for the *Washington Post* who, with Bob Woodward, reported on Watergate as it unfolded. He later coauthored two books with Woodward about Watergate (*All the President's Men*, which was made into a movie, and *The Final Days*). For his role in breaking the story Bernstein received several journalism awards, and his Watergate stories earned the *Post* a Pulitzer prize for public service in 1973. After leaving the *Post* in 1976 Bernstein worked as a senior correspondent for ABC television, taught at New York University, and contributed to *Time* magazine. In 1981 he returned to the *Washington Post* as assistant managing editor for investigations.

Alexander P. Butterfield Butterfield was a former U.S. Air Force pilot who served as a White House aide to President Richard Nixon from 1969 to 1973. In 1972 he was made head of the Federal Aviation Administration. Once the Watergate scandal broke, Butterfield was called before the Senate investigations committee. While giving testimony on July 16, 1973, Butterfield acknowledged that Nixon's Oval Office conversations had been taped, giving the committee reason to request relevant tapes from the president. After serving the Nixon administration Butterfield briefly remained as chief of the Federal Aviation Administration under President Gerald Ford. Butterfield resigned from the post in 1975 to pursue a career as a business executive.

Archibald Cox Cox was a Harvard law professor who in May 1973 was appointed as the first special prosecutor in the Watergate investigation. When the Senate committee investigating Watergate found out that Nixon had recorded his conversations in the Oval Office, Cox pressured the White House to turn over tapes relevant to the investigation. Nixon refused on the grounds that the tapes were privileged executive communications, and he had Cox fired in October 1973 for insisting on their release. Cox later became chairman of the nonprofit group Common Cause. He died of natural causes in 2004.

John Dean Dean was the White House counsel to the president from 1970 to 1973. When the Watergate scandal broke, Dean—under Nixon's direction—worked at covering up the matter. As federal investigations got deeper, he feared the president would make him a scapegoat for the affair so he refused to continue to take part. He was subsequently fired from his post. He was then called before the Senate investigating committee in June 1973 and testified that he, the president, and other aides had conspired to cover up the White House's connection to the burglary and other wrongdoings. He pleaded guilty to obstruction of justice and defrauding the U.S. government; he was sentenced to one to four years in prison, but for cooperating with the investigation his sentence was quickly commuted to time served. After the Watergate affair Dean wrote two memoirs about the scandal called *Blind Ambition* and *Lost Honor*. Today he is an investment banker, author, and public speaker.

John Ehrlichman Ehrlichman served as assistant to the president for domestic affairs under Nixon. He organized the "Plumbers," the group that staged the Watergate break-in, and he fought to suppress leaks about Watergate and fend off threats to the president. When investigations of the scandal eventually led to Ehrlichman and his colleague H.R. Haldeman, Nixon asked for their resignation. In 1975 both men were convicted of conspiracy, obstruction of justice, and perjury for their involvement in Watergate. Ehrlichman served eighteen months in prison for the crimes. After his release he became a writer, artist, political commentator, and author of a book about Watergate called *Witness to Power*. Ehrlichman died in 1999 of complications from diabetes.

Daniel Ellsberg Ellsberg was a former American military analyst turned political activist who became famous in 1971 for releasing the Pentagon Papers, a collection of classified Department of Defense documents describing military activities during the Vietnam War. Because the papers revealed that the government never had a clear plan for winning the war, their release helped build public and congressional opposition to the war. Ellsberg leaked the documents to the *New York Times*, which began printing them in June 1971. He thus earned the enmity of the Nixon administration, which was still pursuing the war, and he was forced to go underground. He eventually surrendered to authorities in June 1973. The Nixon administration, hoping to discredit Ellsberg during his trial, planned and carried out a break-in of the office of Ellsberg's psychiatrist. The break-in became part of the Watergate scandal, since it involved the same team of burglars that subsequently were caught breaking into the Democratic National Committee offices. Ellsberg was later cleared of all charges for his role in releasing the Pentagon Papers. Today he continues to be an activist and public speaker and serves as a senior research associate at the Massachusetts Institute of Technology's Center for International Studies.

Sam J. Ervin Jr. A Democratic U.S. senator from North Carolina from 1954 to 1974, Ervin was the chair of the Senate Select Committee to Investigate Campaign Practices (known as the Senate Watergate committee). He oversaw the actions of the committee as it heard testimony and compiled evidence from May 1973 through June 1974. Ervin resigned from the Senate in 1974 and later practiced law and wrote several books. He died in 1985 from complications of emphysema.

Mark Felt A former agent and top official of the U.S. Federal Bureau of Investigation (FBI), Felt was identified in 2005 as "Deep Throat," the secret government informant to reporters Carl Bernstein and Bob Woodward of the *Washington Post* during the Watergate scandal. Felt, who had known Woodward for some time, fed the reporter tips on who was involved in the cover-up. He published his memoir *The FBI Pyramid from the Inside* in 1979. He was then charged and convicted in

1980 of FBI misdeeds not related to Watergate. He was pardoned by President Ronald Reagan in 1981 for those crimes. He is currently retired.

H.R. (Bob) Haldeman Haldeman was a former advertising executive who helped Nixon win the presidency in 1968. He served as White House chief of staff under Nixon until April 1973, when the president asked him to resign after investigators linked him to the Watergate scandal. One of his conversations with Nixon, just days after the Watergate break-in, was taped by the White House taping system and became the key piece of evidence (the "smoking gun") that convinced Congress to impeach the president and caused Nixon to resign. Along with another White House aide, John Ehrlichman, Haldeman was convicted of conspiracy, obstruction of justice, and perjury for his involvement in Watergate. He served eighteen months in prison. Later, he became a successful real estate developer and entrepreneur. In 1978 he wrote a book called *The Ends of Power* in which he took responsibility for creating a pressurized atmosphere in the White House that helped to create the Watergate scandal. Haldeman died of undisclosed causes in 1993. In 1994, diaries of his White House years were published as *The Haldeman Diaries*.

E. Howard Hunt Hunt was a White House consultant and a member of the "Plumbers," a secret White House investigation unit set up by White House aide John Ehrlichman to spy on and discredit Democrats and other political enemies of the president. Hunt's phone number was found in a notebook belonging to one of the Watergate burglars, and he and another Plumbers member, G. Gordon Liddy, pleaded guilty to directing the Watergate break-in. Hunt was sentenced to two-and-a-half to eight years in prison and a ten-thousand-dollar fine, but he was released from prison after serving thirty-three months. Later, he became an author and lecturer. He currently writes spy novels.

Leon Jaworski Jaworski was a Houston lawyer who was appointed to replace Special Prosecutor Archibald Cox after Nixon fired Cox. Jaworski accepted the appointment only after receiving assurances that he could conduct an independent investigation and take the president to court if necessary. Jaworski requested access to more than sixty-four presidential tapes, and the legal case he mounted reached the U.S. Supreme Court in July 1974. The Court's order that the president turn over the tapes was the critical event that exposed Nixon's involvement in Watergate. After Watergate, Jaworski served as treasurer of Democrats for Reagan in the 1980 presidential election. He died of a heart attack in 1982.

Richard Kleindienst After serving under Nixon first as deputy attorney general and then as attorney general, Kleindienst resigned in the midst of the Watergate scandal in April 1973, along with White House aides H.R. Haldeman and John Erlichman and White House counsel John Dean. Kleindienst was convicted of a misdemeanor for perjury in his congressional testimony during Watergate, for which he was fined and given a suspended jail sentence. He later returned to private law practice. He died of lung cancer in 2000.

G. Gordon Liddy Along with E. Howard Hunt, Liddy was part of the "Plumbers," a special investigative unit set up by White House aide John Ehrlichman to spy on and discredit Nixon's political enemies. Both Liddy and Hunt were convicted of conspiracy, burglary, and illegal wiretapping in relation to the Watergate break-in. Liddy was sentenced to twenty years in prison for his crimes, but was released after serving only four years. Following his time in prison Liddy became an actor, author, and host of a widely syndicated radio talk show that focuses on political topics.

James W. McCord Jr. A former Central Intelligence Agency (CIA) employee and security coordinator for Nixon's reelection committee, McCord was one of the five men arrested for the Watergate burglary (along with Bernard Barker, Virgilio González, Eugenio Martínez, and Frank Sturgis). He pled guilty to charges of conspiracy, burglary, and wiretapping for his role in Watergate. In March 1973, while awaiting sentencing, McCord wrote a letter to Judge John J. Sirica stating that high-level White House officials had pressured the Watergate defendants to plead guilty. Because of his cooperation, he served only sixty-nine days of a one-to-five-year prison sentence. In 1974 McCord wrote a book about Watergate called *A Piece of Tape: The Watergate Story: Fact and Fiction.* He later became a booster for the University of Michigan Athletic Department.

John N. Mitchell A former law partner of Nixon's, Mitchell served as attorney general from 1969 to 1972 during Nixon's first term as president. In 1972 he became head of the president's reelection committee, a position he held when the Watergate scandal broke. He was convicted of conspiracy, obstruction of justice, and perjury for his role in Watergate, and sentenced to two-and-a-half to eight years in prison. Mitchell was released from prison after serving nineteen months. After leaving prison he joined an international consulting business with another Nixon aide. He died in 1988 of a heart attack.

Elliot Richardson Richardson was appointed by Nixon to replace Attorney General Richard Kleindienst, who resigned in April 1973 in the midst of the Watergate scandal. In October 1973 Richardson himself resigned rather than comply with an order from Nixon to fire Special Prosecutor Archibald Cox. Following Watergate, Richardson served as secretary of the Department of Commerce and ambassador to Britain under President Gerald Ford. In 1998 he was awarded the Presidential Medal of Freedom, the nation's highest civilian honor, for his role in Watergate. Richardson died in 1999.

William D. Ruckelshaus Ruckelshaus served as deputy U.S. attorney general under Nixon. Along with Attorney General Elliot Richardson, he resigned in 1973 rather than comply with Nixon's order to fire Special Prosecutor Archibald Cox. After Watergate, Ruckelshaus returned to private law practice. Since then he has served in many important government positions as well as on the boards of several private companies and nonprofit organizations.

John J. Sirica At the time of the Watergate burglary, Sirica was the chief judge of the U.S. District Court for the District of Columbia. He presided over the trials of the Watergate defendants and ordered Nixon to produce presidential tape recordings to Watergate prosecutors. His ruling on the tapes was appealed all the way to the U.S. Supreme Court and resulted in the Court's June 24, 1974, order that Nixon release all requested tapes. Sirica retired from the bench in 1986. He died in 1992.

Frank Wills Wills was the security guard at the Watergate apartment and office complex, where, on June 17, 1972, he discovered that burglars had broken into the office complex. After police responded to Wills's call, five men were arrested for illegally entering the Democratic National Committee headquarters, which occupied one of the offices. These events precipitated the Watergate scandal. Wills died of complications from a brain tumor in 2000.

Bob Woodward Woodward was an investigative reporter for the *Washington Post* who, along with Carl Bernstein, reported on the Watergate scandal as it unfolded. Woodward later co-authored two books with Bernstein about Watergate (*All the President's Men* and *The Final Days*). Today, Woodward serves as assistant managing editor for the *Washington Post* and is one of the most famous and respected contemporary journalists. He has won many accolades and awards for his reporting, including two Pulitzer prizes. Over the years he also has written twelve best-selling nonfiction books.

Chronology

June 17, 1972

Five men are caught breaking into the offices of the Democratic National Committee at the Watergate apartment and office complex. One is James W. McCord Jr., security director for the Committee to Reelect the President (CRP).

June 23, 1972

Nixon approves a plan to interfere with the FBI investigation of the Watergate break-in; the conversation is secretly taped by the president.

September 15, 1972

The five Watergate burglars and two others, G. Gordon Liddy and E. Howard Hunt, are indicted in a federal district court.

November 7, 1972

Nixon is reelected president by a huge margin.

January 8, 1973

The trial of the Watergate burglars begins. Five of the defendants change their pleas from innocent to guilty during the trial. McCord and Liddy are convicted on January 30.

February 7, 1973

The Senate votes to establish a Select Committee on Presidential Campaign Activities. The committee, also known as the Watergate Committee, is chaired by Sen. Sam J. Ervin Jr., a Democrat from North Carolina.

March 21, 1973

White House counsel John Dean tells Nixon that there is a "cancer" growing on the presidency.

March 23, 1973

A letter by McCord to Judge John J. Sirica is read by Sirica in open court; McCord charges that the defendants had pleaded guilty under pressure and that perjury was committed at the trial.

April 6, 1973

Dean begins negotiations regarding his cooperating with federal Watergate prosecutors.

April 17, 1973

Presidential press secretary Ronald L. Ziegler says that all previous White House statements on Watergate are "inoperative."

April 30, 1973

Nixon announces the dismissal of Dean and the resignations of top aides H.R. Haldeman and John Ehrlichman. Attorney General Richard Kleindienst also resigns and is replaced by Elliot Richardson.

May 18, 1973

Richardson appoints Archibald Cox to be special prosecutor for the Watergate case.

May–October 1973

The Senate Watergate committee holds public televised hearings.

June 25, 1973

Dean testifies before the Watergate committee; he describes a political espionage program conducted by the White House and asserts that Nixon was involved in the cover-up of the Watergate break-in.

July 16, 1973

White House aide Alexander P. Butterfield, testifying before the Senate Watergate committee, reveals the existence of a White House taping system.

July 25, 1973

Nixon refuses to release White House tapes to Cox, arguing that such a concession would jeopardize the "independence of the three branches of government."

October 10, 1973

Vice President Spiro Agnew resigns in the face of tax evasion and other charges unrelated to the Watergate scandal.

October 12, 1973

Nixon nominates Gerald R. Ford to replace Agnew as vice president.

October 20, 1973

The "Saturday Night Massacre" occurs; Nixon orders Richardson to fire Cox. Richardson refuses and resigns. The deputy attorney general is dismissed after refusing to fire Cox. Finally, Solicitor General Robert Bork dismisses the special prosecutor.

October 23, 1973

Nixon agrees to release the tapes Cox had sought.

October 30, 1973

The House Judiciary Committee begins consideration of possible impeachment proceedings.

November 1, 1973

Nixon appoints Leon Jaworski the new Watergate special prosecutor.

November 21, 1973

The public learns that one of the tapes Cox wanted has a mysterious eighteen-and-a-half minute gap in it.

February 6, 1974

The House votes to proceed with a Nixon impeachment inquiry and gives the House Judiciary Committee broad subpoena powers.

February 25, 1974

In a nationally televised speech, Nixon vows never to resign from office.

March 1, 1974

A federal grand jury indicts Haldeman, Ehrlichman, John Mitchell, Gordon Strachan, Robert Mardian, Kenneth Parkinson, and Charles Colson for covering up the Watergate burglary; Nixon is named as an unindicted coconspirator.

April 30, 1974

Nixon releases more edited transcripts of tapes, which are noteworthy for their frankness and for adding the phrase "expletive deleted" to the nation's vocabulary.

May 7, 1974

Nixon's lawyer, James D. St. Clair, announces that no more White House tapes will be turned over to the special prosecutor or the House Judiciary Committee.

May 9, 1974

The House Judiciary Committee begins impeachment hearings.

July 24, 1974

The U.S. Supreme Court rules 8-0 in *United States v. Nixon* that the president must turn over the White House tapes requested by Jaworski.

July 27–30, 1974

The House Judiciary Committee votes to recommend three articles of impeachment against Nixon.

August 5, 1974

The "smoking gun" tape from June 23, 1972, is released to the public; it reveals that Nixon was part of the Watergate cover-up early on.

August 8, 1974

Nixon announces his resignation from office, effective noon the next day.

August 9, 1974

Gerald Ford becomes the nation's thirty-eighth president.

September 8, 1974

Ford gives Nixon a "full, free, and absolute pardon" for whatever crimes the former president may have committed.

May 31, 2005

The *Washington Post* confirms that former FBI agent Mark Felt was "Deep Throat," the secret source used by *Post* reporters Bob Woodward and Carl Bernstein during their coverage of the Watergate scandal in the 1970s.

For Further Research

Books on Watergate

Carl Bernstein and Bob Woodward, *All the President's Men.* New York: Simon and Schuster, 1974.

Daniel Cohen, *Watergate: Deception in the White House.* Brookfield, CT: Millbrook, 1998.

Len Colodny and Robert Gettlin, *Silent Coup: The Removal of Richard Nixon.* New York: St. Martin's, 1990.

Elizabeth Drew, *Washington Journal: The Events of 1973–1974.* New York: Random House, 1975.

Mark E. Dudley, *United States v. Nixon (1974): Presidential Powers.* New York: Twenty-First Century, 1994.

Fred Emery, *Watergate: The Corruption of American Politics and the Fall of Richard Nixon.* New York: Times Books, 1994.

Barbara Silberdick Feinberg, *Watergate: Scandal in the White House.* New York: Franklin Watts, 1990.

David K. Fremon, *The Watergate Scandal in American History.* Springfield, NJ: Enslow, 1998.

Michael A. Genovese, *The Watergate Crisis.* Westport, CT: Greenwood, 1999.

Jeff Hay, ed., *Richard M. Nixon: Presidents and Their Decisions.* San Diego: Greenhaven, 2001.

Stanley I. Kutler, *The Wars of Watergate: The Last Crisis of Richard Nixon.* New York: Knopf, 1990.

Stanley I. Kutler, ed., *Abuse of Power: The New Nixon Tapes.* New York: Touchstone, 1998.

Victor Lasky, *It Didn't Start with Watergate.* New York: Dial, 1977.

J. Anthony Lukas, *Nightmare: The Underside of the Nixon Years*. New York: Penguin, 1988.

Kim McQuaid, *The Anxious Years: America in the Vietnam-Watergate Era*. New York: BasicBooks, 1989.

Richard Nixon, *RN: The Memory of Richard Nixon*. New York: Grosset and Dunlop, 1978.

Myron J. Smith, *Watergate: An Annotated Bibliography of Sources in English, 1972–1982*. Metuchen, NJ: Scarecrow, 1983.

Political Cartoon Books

Amon Carter Museum of Western Art, *The Image of America in Caricature and Cartoon*. Fort Worth, TX: Amon Carter Museum of Western Art, 1976.

Tony Auth, *Behind the Lines*. Boston: Houghton Mifflin, 1977.

Herbert Block, *Herblock Special Report*. New York: Norton, 1974.

Paul Conrad, *The King and Us*. Los Angeles: Clymer, 1974.

Jules Feiffer, *Feiffer on Nixon: The Cartoon Presidency*. New York: Random House, 1974.

Roger A. Fischer, *Them Damned Pictures: Explorations in American Political Cartoon Art*. North Haven, CT: Archon, 1996.

Ranan R. Lurie, *Nixon-Rated Cartoons*. New York: Quadrangle, 1974.

Mike Peters, *The Nixon Chronicles*. Dayton, OH: Lorenz, 1976.

Paul P. Somers Jr., *Editorial Cartooning and Caricature: A Reference Guide*. Westport, CT: Greenwood, 1998.

G.B. Trudeau, *Guilty, Guilty, Guilty! A Doonesbury Book*. New York: Holt, Rinehart, and Winston, 1974.

Web Sites

Caroline and Erwin Swann Collection of Caricature and Cartoon. (http://www.loc.gov/rr/print/coll/230_swan.html). The Web site is associated with a collection of caricatures and cartoons that was donated to the Library of Congress in 1977. It includes a searchable catalog of cartoon images and a listing of other library and online cartoon collections.

Illusion and Delusion: The Watergate Decade. (www.journale .com/watergate). This is an online photograph essay of the Watergate era that includes portraits of key players in the scandal.

Nixon Tapes. (www.nara.gov/nixon/tapes/index.html). In this Web site the National Archives and Records Adminstration (NARA) provides public access to 1,284 hours of the tapes President Nixon recorded.

Watergate. (http://vcepolitics.com/watergate). Constructed by an Australian political science teacher, this Web site provides a chronological overview of Watergate and links to speeches and other primary sources.

Watergate 25th Aniversary. (www.cnn.com/ALLPOLITICS/ 1997/gen/resources/watergate/sites.html). This Web site, a coproduction of Cable News Network (CNN) and *Time* magazine, contains numerous links to articles, photographs, timelines, political cartoons, presidential transcripts, and other Watergate Web sites.

Index